Fast Lanes

Other Books By Frederick C. Klein

The Education of a Horseplayer (with Sam Lewin)
News and the Market (with John Prestbo)
Lem Banker's Book of Sports Betting (with Lem Banker)
Bulls, Bears and Other Sports (editor)
On Sports

"Fast Lanes ;

Carmen Salvino and professional bowling grew up together—here is their story [by]

Carmen Salvino *with* Frederick C. Klein ,

Bonus Books, Chicago
[c1988]

92 91 90 89 88   5 4 3

Library of Congress Catalog Card Number: 87-73002

International Standard Book Number: 0-933893-46-9

Bonus Books, Inc.
160 East Illinois Street
Chicago, Illinois 60611

Printed in the United States of America

To my wife, Ginny, who has given me the help, support and love that I have needed in this roller coaster life of mine. I couldn't have made it without you, and I love you deeply.

To my daughter, Corinne, a chip off the old block, who has made a joy of the responsibility of being a father.

To my son-in-law, Pat, a man I could not love more if he were my own flesh and blood.

C.S.

Contents

Acknowledgements

Thanks to Roger Tessman, Bert Kellerman and Dave DeLorenzo of the American Bowling Congress, for providing background materials for this book. Thanks to Tom Kouros of Rand-River Bowl, a skilled bowling teacher and writer, for helping me put into words some of the bowling techniques that seemed to just "come naturally" to me in practice.

Thanks to Remo Picchietti, of DBA Products Co., for technical assistance in the area of lane surfaces. Thanks to Bill Lieber, John Bergmann and Paul Marcinek, of Leiber's Pro Shop in Chicago, for advice on the selection of bowling equipment and the use of their shop.

Thanks to Lyle Zikes, Chuck Pezzano and Joe Panko, Jr., for refreshing my memory about the early days of the Professional Bowlers Association tour. Thanks to Susie

Klein for her help in preparing the manuscript of this book, and Natalie Hector for her prompt and efficient work in transcribing interview tapes. Thanks to John Gaski for teaching me to play gin rummy.

Thanks, too, to the following people, who have been there for me when I've needed them: The Salvino family, especially my brother, Joe; Eddie Elias, Jim Troxell, Jim Stefanich, Ed Dong, Tom Horiike, Bill Moore, Dean Courtade, Joe Antenora; Lou Caras and Earl Filskov of Riveria Lanes; Bob Habetler of Habetler Bowl; Tom Malloy, Bill Supper and Andy Lee of Ebonite International Inc.; Art Jonas, Tom Kicher, Bob Diderly; Tom Czajka, John Allen and Dan Edwards of Amoco Chemical Co.; the Salachs, Ladd, Ken and Gary; and George and Gene Chioles.

C.S.

Preface

It is 8:30 on a January Friday morning in Chicago, which is to say that it is gray, cold and blustery. Worse yet, it's beginning to snow. Still, Carmen Salvino, who has been a professional bowler for 36 of his 53 years, and has been elected to more halls of fame than most people have credit cards, is up and out for a between-tournaments practice session at Habetler Bowl on the city's low-rise Northwest Side. The place was built by Rudy Habetler, the American Bowling Congress's Masters champion of 1953, whom Salvino once dueled in the old Chicago Classic League. Now it's run by Rudy's son, Bob.

Habetler's hasn't opened yet, so Salvino rattles its glass-and-metal door. Curtis, a thin young maintenance man, eventually appears to let him in. Salvino greets him. He also hellos Nancy, a besmocked employee who is picking up beer bottles and other debris from the night before.

"I'm going for coffee. Want me to bring you some?" Salvino hollers to both. They nod in the negative, so he deposits his two tan, double-ball bowling bags inside the door and leaves with a friend for the Blue Angel restaurant across the street, seeking breakfast.

The Blue Angel is large and mostly empty; its bandstand indicates that it doubles as a supperclub at night, or used to. A middle-aged blonde hostess shows Salvino to a booth. She inquires about his health, and he asks about hers. He has been coming here for years.

Salvino orders a Denver omelette and decaffeinated coffee. "You gotta make *some* concessions to age," he says in reference to the latter. He doesn't make many, though. "I feel as good today as I did 10, 15, 20 years ago. I really do," he says between mouthfuls. "I watch what I eat, I exercise, and I bowl just about every day. Hey, if somebody tells you that professional bowlers aren't athletes, you tell him he's all wet. I swing that 16-pound ball maybe 200 times in my average practice session. Let some baseball or football player try that. Every muscle on his bowling-arm side would be aching, and he'd be walking lopsided for a week."

By nine o'clock Salvino is back at Habetler's, stripping off his topcoat, scarf and brown sweater to reveal a brown-and-orange pullover shirt and brown slacks. He's color-coordinated even when he practices. It's part of the tidy image that professional bowling projects, and it has helped make the sport television's biggest underground attraction, out-rating golf, tennis, run-of-the-ring boxing, hockey and even basketball. That bowling topples those other sports on the tube year in and year out always comes as a surprise to the upscale types who fancy that they determine national tastes.

Out of the tan bags come Salvino's white bowling shoes

and four bowling balls, which differ slightly in composition and feel. Three of the balls are of his own design, made with chemical formulas he has devised and weight blocks that are placed differently from those of conventional balls. Salvino began the study of chemistry and physics under the tutelage of the late Hank Lahr, an engineer and long-time friend who helped resuscitate his career years before. The bowling part of the project entailed a total remake of Salvino's style of delivery. It succeeded so well that, at age 40, he became a winner again on the Professional Bowlers Association tour after a four-year drought. "Before I got with Hank I did things by instinct, like a typical jock," Salvino says. "He made me break down everything I was doing so that I really understood it, and then we put it all back together again in a different way. It opened up a whole new way of looking at things for me. Not just at bowling—everything!"

The mental discipline Salvino acquired in that process propelled him into scientific projects of his own. He has only a high-school diploma, but he now holds a patent for a bowling-ball weight-block design, and has developed chemical compounds not only for the manufacture of bowling balls but also for a non-skid concrete that might be used in highway bridges. When (if?) he retires from the bowling tour, his royalty income should keep him warm.

Except for Salvino and the few employees, Habetler Bowl is empty, and still cold from the nighttime thermostat turndown. Salvino blows on his hands to warm them, selects a dull-black ball from among the four on the rack (as a rule, dull balls grip the lanes better than the shiny ones many people use) and assumes his stance behind the foul line, his left foot slightly ahead of his right.

Salvino is a tall man, standing about six-feet-two and

weighing a trim 185 pounds. His hair is partly gray and thin-nish on top, but he has the sloping shoulders, long arms and erect carriage of an athlete. Besides his long nose, his most striking feature (no pun intended) is his right hand. It is large, with thick fingers that widen, not taper, at the ends, the effect of releasing millions of bowling balls over 40 years. He has a hand grip that can crush walnuts.

He allows the ball to hang straight down his right side and takes four short steps forward—right–left–right–left—swinging the ball back and outward in a powerful arc. It starts just to the right of center-lane, swings toward the right gutter (oops, they're "channels" now) and hooks into the 1-3 pin pocket. With a crash made startling by the silence it breaks, the pins explode for a strike.

Salvino throws three more strikes and then turns and smiles. "Just warmin' up," he says. Once, in practice, he threw 51 consecutive strikes, and he threw 26 in a row in a tournament. At the 1980 Professional Bowlers Association of America (PBA) National Championship in Sterling Heights, Michigan, he scored a record 4,015 for a 16-game set, an average of 251 a game. In 1952, when he was 19 years old, he and partner Joe Wilman won the Bowling Pro-prietors Association of America (BPAA) national doubles tourney. In 1984, at age 51, he took the PBA National Seniors crown. He has knocked down more pins in and cashed more checks from PBA tournaments than any other man, and has taken home enough trophies to stock a good-sized sporting goods store.

This string of strikes does not last; his next ball leaves the 10-pin standing. Instead of going for the spare, however, he pushes the button on the ball-return stand that causes the automatic pinsetter to remove the pin and reset the full ten. He rarely practices spares because they require a different throwing motion from his ''strike'' ball, and he doesn't want to disturb his rhythm with a PBA event approaching. ''You don't cash on the tour against the best bowlers in the world by grinding out 190 scores. You aim for strings of six or seven strikes and those 230s or 240s,'' he explains. ''You know you're in trouble in a tournament if you're leaving spares to pick up.''

As the session wears on, strikes become more elusive. At one point, he puts a white-tape tracer on his ball to better observe its spin. ''Too flat,'' he murmurs. He makes adjustments in his delivery to improve his ball's motion.

His next move is to change bowling balls, something he also does during tournaments when conditions warrant it. He observes that many people, including some novice bowlers, think of bowling as a game of static conditions, but that nothing could be further from the truth. ''When the average guy looks down a bowling lane, he sees ten pins set up 60 feet away, period. That's not what I see,'' he says. ''I see the wear left by other people's balls. I see dry patches here and there. I see oil conditions that change from day to day and even hour to hour as oil from the front of the lane gravitates toward the rear. The same ball that's solid in the pocket in frame one can miss the headpin altogether by the end of the game if a player doesn't make the right adjustments.

''Friends of mine who play golf tell me that bowling is easy—that it's the same old stuff, over and over. I tell 'em *they* have it easy. When they're sizing up a hole, they can see the trees and water holes and sand traps right out there, and get down on their knees and feel the grain of the green. We gotta put up with the same kind of obstacles, only ours are a whole lot more difficult to spot.''

Then it is back to practice, ball after ball. Absent are the balletic leaps and spins that punctuate his performances in tournament play. That is for the crowd, and there is none here yet this day. No score is kept, for that, too, would be a distraction.

At about ten o'clock, the center begins to fill with women arriving for league play. They chatter, laugh, drink coffee from plastic cups, cheer one another's strikes, and groan over missed spares. Some occasionally glance toward the tall man bowling alone at the far end of the row of lanes, and a few clearly recognize him. But no one interrupts for talk or autographs. There is, apparently, a code about such things here.

At about 10:30, Salvino's lean, blonde wife of 31 years, Ginny, arrives. "Hi, coach," he smiles, and she smiles back. That's a joke, but only partly. Ginny was an accomplished amateur bowler, and often accompanies her husband to practices and tournaments. She knows more about his delivery and habits than anybody.

"Watch me a couple of times, willya hon? Something's not quite right," Carmen says. He throws a few balls and looks to her for comment.

"You're too high," she says.

"No I'm not. I think the trouble is my first step. I feel like I'm jamming it instead of moving smooth."

She disagrees and moves closer to him. Their exchanges become more heated and rapid. Carmen begins to gesture. He looks perturbed. Ginny sits down and Carmen throws a few more balls. The last two are strikes. "The jam step pulled me up. That's why I came off high," he says. Both smile. It's a familiar sequence. Score another one for marital harmony.

A dozen or so more balls and Salvino finds a groove that pleases him. He fires four straight strikes, and on the last whirls across the empty lane to his right in the sort of gesture that has become his trademark. One's company, two's an audience. Besides, he feels like it.

It is now 11:20 and he has been on the lanes without pause for well over two hours. That's more bowling than the average league player does in a month, and a decent day's labor by any reckoning. It's only the beginning of Salvino's working day, though.

From Habetler's on West Foster Avenue, he drives his maroon Cadillac south to his home neighborhood, pausing for a corned-beef-sandwich lunch along the way. His next stop is at Hal Lieber's Pro Shop, a bowling supplies store on North Avenue, where he keeps and works on the 25 or so balls he is testing as part of a program by a major manufacturer to market a line of balls using compositions and balancing principles he has developed. He dons an apron and spends the best part of an hour at the large drill press in the shop, drilling holes in the balls to fit his thumb and finger measurements. Using a heat lamp on his work bench to warm them, he tests the balls for hardness at various temperatures, and carefully notes the results. Later in the week, he'll take the balls out on the lanes.

"That's where I've got it over the other scientists," he says. "They can only do calculations; I can formulate a ball and then go out and see how it performs. When I tell them a certain ball hooks this much, and another ball hooks only that much, they can take it to the bank. One-stop bowling engineering, that's me. I'm unique in the industry."

On his way out, Salvino stops to chat with Paul Marcinek, a young employee of the store. "What are people buying?" he asks.

"Balls that hook—the more the better," says Marcinek.

"That's good," says Salvino. "Nobody's ball is going to hook better than the one I'm making."

Then it's home to the comfortable, second-floor apartment on a quiet Northwest Side street that Carmen and Ginny have occupied for 25 years. Their daughter, Corinne, is grown and married, and is a computer-software specialist. There he will spend the remaining afternoon hours on his ball designs, filling notebook upon notebook with penciled calculations. Boxes of them compete with bowling trophies for space in the spare bedroom he uses as an office.

His chosen game, he muses, is a lot more complicated than it was when, as a 17 year old, he couldn't wait to get out of Crane Tech High School on Chicago's West Side so he could roll bowling balls all day. "You learn a little, and pretty soon you want to learn a lot. And when you do, you discover how little you really know," he says with a laugh. "But, hey, I threw a lifetime worth of strikes before I turned 25. If it weren't for complications, I'd have quit bowling long ago. You never know; maybe I'd even have taken up golf."

Frederick C. Klein

1

The First Frame

One of my clearest early memories is about
something that happened to me as a kid of five
years old in Dania, Florida, which is about
20 miles north of Miami. Me and my parents
and two brothers were living there, working
on my grandfather's farm. When I say we
were poor, I'm not just being dramatic. We
lived on the top floor of a two-story wooden
apartment building that was more like a barracks than any city apartment. There was no
electricity or indoor plumbing. My mom
cooked on a wood-burning stove that also
provided whatever heat we'd have in the place
on cold nights. I owned just one, banged-up
pair of shoes, and in the summer I mostly went
barefoot. My brothers did, too.

One day my folks sent me to Dania's little
shopping street, which was about a half-mile
from where we lived, to pick up our mail at
the post office. As I was walking along, I saw

something shiny laying in a ditch alongside the road. It was a cracked, wooden bowling pin. There were a couple of outdoor bowling lanes on the edge of town, under a tent, and I guess someone from there threw it away after it had been broken.

I'd never been bowling, or even seen anyone bowl, and didn't know what the thing in the ditch was. But I liked its shape and its painted-white finish. I took it home and put it in the room I shared with my brothers. I didn't have many toys, so I used it as one. I'd set it up and kick it over, or throw rocks or other things at it. When we moved back to Chicago a year later, I took it with me, and I still had it when we all moved back to Florida a few years after that. It got lost somewhere, I can't remember when. That's too bad, because I'd like to have it as a memento of those years.

I guess I remember that story particularly because it was one of the few nice things that happened to me as a child. It seemed that we were always poor and always moving between Chicago, where I was born in the Depression year of 1933, and South Florida. And we were always working very hard.

As I put it together from stories I've been told, my forebears were Italian farmers from the province of Calabria, in southern Italy. My grandfather came to America as a young man. His name was Carmen, too; I'm named after him. He died when I was young, and I don't recall much about him, except that I didn't like him very much. I remember once, in Dania, when I was five or six years old, I told him I wanted to make some money. He told me that if I went out in the fields and picked some vegetables, he'd pay me. I took a big sack and picked for what seemed like hours. When I hauled the sack home and gave it to him, he laughed and gave me some paper play money. I was wise enough to know the money was phony, and it made me angry. Another thing about him I didn't like was that he'd tease me about taking back my name if I didn't behave right.

Speaking of my name, I must admit that I had hangups about it when I was younger, from the time I heard about the opera *Carmen*. That Carmen was a Spanish woman, and I got to thinking that I might be walking around with a woman's name. Then someone told me that "Carmine" was the masculine form of the name, and it occurred to me that maybe my parents couldn't spell so good. As I got older, though, I heard about other guys named Carmen, including Carmen Cavalero, the pianist, and Carmen Basilio, the champion boxer, and I decided that maybe it wasn't such a bad name after all. I guess how the name is spelled depends on what part of Italy your people came from.

My father's name is Michael, and he's still going strong at more than 80 years of age. He left his father's farm in Dania to try to find work in Chicago after he married my mother, Theresa. Both Mom and Dad had relatives in Chicago, and they helped some. But Dad had only a third-grade education, and no real skills, so he always had a tough time earning a living. He was a big man—six-foot-two and 210 or 220 pounds—and very strong. When he'd hit me, I'd see stars. As I think back, that happened pretty often, because he wasn't much for talking to us boys about what we should or shouldn't do. When he caught me or my brothers doing something he didn't like, it was "Whack!" across the head, and we didn't do it again. Or, at least, we didn't do it while he was watching.

I was the second of four children. The eldest, Joe, is three years older than me, and my other brother, Richard, is 11 months younger. Our sister, Phyllis, is 12 years younger than I am, so she didn't grow up with us boys.

From a physical standpoint, Richard and I most resemble Dad, although Richard is the closest. I'm more on the lean side. Joe is shorter and lighter, and probably the most graceful. As a young man, he was always very conscious of his appearance. He lifted weights before many other guys were into that, and he always dressed nice. He was a great dancer; he and a partner won the big Harvest Moon dance contest in the Chicago Stadium one year, and he later performed as a professional dancer. After that he did some clothes modeling. He sells aluminum now. Richard is an electrician, and Phyllis is a housewife and mother.

I'm closest in age to Richard, but hung around more with Joe when we were boys. I really can't say why that was. Maybe there was too much rivalry between Richard and me, our ages being so close. All the time we were growing up, Joe, Richard and I slept in the same bed. We'd get up in the morning, and, right away, Richard and I would duke it out until Joe or Dad or Mom could get between us. Then, one morning when we were 12 or 13 years old, Richard and I woke up, looked at each other, and broke out laughing. We didn't fight again after that, and became better friends.

It was a good thing that my brothers and I got along, because we didn't have too many other friends. That's because of all the moving we did between Chicago and Florida. We left Chicago the first time when I was five years old to go to grandfather Carmen's farm in Dania. I remember packing everything we owned into an old pickup truck—furniture, pots and pans, clothes and mattresses—and heading south, with me riding on top of the mattresses in back. We were like the Joads in that book, *The Grapes of Wrath*. I really, really didn't want to go, and cried all the way.

We stayed in Dania for two years, but prices for the vegetables we grew dropped so low that the farm couldn't support the whole bunch of us, so it was back to Chicago and the neighborhood around Flournoy and Laflin Streets where we'd lived before. We were home for two years— then like now I considered Chicago my real home—but the only work Dad would get was as a street repair man with the government's Work Progress Administration, or WPA, where you had to be poor to qualify to work and got food stamps along with money for pay. If you worked on WPA, you weren't supposed to have extra cash to spend. My mother once bought me a nickel candy bar at a store, and a government spotter caught her and asked her a lot of questions about where she got the money. That was what life was like during the Depression.

Chicago and WPA work weren't good, either, so Dad figured he would try his hand at farming on his own. He leased about 20 acres of land near Davie, Florida, which was a few miles west, or inland, of Dania. It was the same scene all over again: same old pickup truck, clothes, furniture and other stuff in the back, and me on top of the mattresses. I was too old to cry this time—I was nine—but I remember having a stomach ache all the way to Florida.

Being older, I remember a lot more about our place in Davie than the one in Dania. Instead of the sort of barracks apartment we had before, we lived in a couple of little wooden houses. Actually, they were more like shacks. We cooked and ate in one shack and slept in the other. We still had an outdoor water pump and an outhouse-toilet that smelled awful, but at least this place had an orange tree in the backyard that was pretty and gave us some good fruit.

I was in school by then, but every daylight minute I wasn't there I was out working. Our farm had earth that was so soft it was like muck. Any trucks or machinery you drove out on it would sink to the axles, and we had no barn in which to keep draft animals. That meant that all the planting, weeding and harvesting had to be done by hand. Joe, me, Richard, Dad and Mom were out in the fields every day, doing one thing or another. The weather usually was hot, and the only water we had was what we could carry. Mom was a small woman, and the work was particularly rough on her. She changed physically during our years in Davie, just kind of wearing out. She died in 1986, at the age of 80, but was never as healthy or lively as she was before we went there.

I don't know which part of the farm work I disliked most, planting or harvesting. Because of the soft earth, we had to pull the plow ourselves, taking turns being the "horse." Believe me, that was difficult. Of all the things we grew, harvesting potatoes was the worst. They grow underneath the surface where you can't see them, and you couldn't risk bruising them with hand tools. You stuck your hands into the ground and groped around for them, and you'd run into stones and pieces of wood and parts of old roots. Stuff was always getting stuck under our fingernails. There were many nights when my mother would have to sit up with us, pulling splinters and other things out with tweezers. We used to cut our hands a lot, and being in dirt all the time meant we had lots of infections. I can't recall many days in Davie that I wasn't bandaged.

At harvest time, which is pretty much most of the year on a truck farm in the sunny South, work didn't stop at sunset.

At night, we'd gather at the pump behind the house the vegetables we'd picked during the day, wash them in tubs, and pack them in boxes. I remember washing vegetables around those little light bulbs we had (at least that place had electricity), with flies and gnats buzzing all around.

My father would drive the truck into Miami to sell the vegetables, and sometimes I or my brothers would go with him. We'd have to leave at night to get a decent stall at the farmer's market, and sometimes we wouldn't get back to Davie until two mornings later. A lot of times we'd come home without selling everything we brought. Then we'd have to eat the leftovers ourselves. It made for good meals for a couple of days, but they were spoiled by the knowledge that, without cash, we wouldn't be able to pay our bills the next month.

The days we boys didn't work on our own farm, we hired out to others in the neighborhood. Joe, Richard and I cut and loaded sod for a couple of brothers named Griffith. We'd put in 10 to 14 hours a day, and never earned more than two dollars each for it. We'd also pick and crate oranges all day for the same two bucks. It seemed that we earned two dollars a day no matter what we did, or for whom. I guess the bigger farmers in that area got together and established that as the standard daily wage. Looked at another way, though, money didn't matter much to the Salvino brothers, because we had to turn over everything we earned to Mom and Dad. That was the rule in the house for all of us until we had grown up and moved away.

You might think that such an upbringing would make a person mercenary, but it didn't turn out that way with me. Money never has been one of my major concerns. I can recall my scores from bowling tournaments of 20 or 30 years ago, and the names of guys that I've hustled, but I'm always hard-pressed to remember the size of the checks I've cashed. Once, after I won an event on the PBA tour, I even forgot to pick up my winnings before leaving the bowling center. I'm always stuffing checks in my pockets and forgetting about them. My wife, Ginny, finds them when she does the laundry or takes my clothes to the cleaners. She says that if it wasn't for her, I'd have lost about half of the prize money I've won over the years.

All our hard work in Davie went for naught, though. What did us in was the failure of our tomato crop our last year there. Tomatoes were fetching a pretty good price then—I think it was about eight dollars a bushel—and we'd planted 10 acres of them, about half our farm. We were within a few days of harvest time when a sudden frost came up and killed them all—shriveled them right up. I'd never seen Dad even flinch over anything before, but that night he sat down and cried.

So it was back to Chicago for us, and for good, as it turned out. It was 1944, with World War II on, and jobs were easier to get than before we'd left. Dad caught on in construction, and he stayed in that for the better part of his working life. Mostly, he ran those jackhammer machines that broke up the streets and sidewalks. He'd run them all day, and when he'd get home at night he couldn't hear what we were saying because the machines messed up his ears so bad. But at least he was finally earning a living wage.

For the Salvino brothers, being home in Chicago was great. Moving around a lot isn't easy on kids, and we'd spent our early lives being strangers wherever we went. In the South, we were "Yankees," and in Chicago, we were "farmers.'' Still, Chicago was a big city, with lots of things to do and different guys to hang around with. It was a better deal by far than small-town Florida, we thought.

This is not to say that we had it easy in the Big Town. Back in our old apartment at Flournoy and Laflin Streets, Joe, Richard and I still slept three to a bed, just like in Davie. You get pretty close to your brothers that way. And we still had to go out and work after school and turn the money over to our folks. I did just about everything a kid could do to earn a buck, including delivering groceries, shining shoes and selling newspapers. I sold papers for about a year at a stand on the corner of Randolph and Clark Streets downtown. After pulling a plow in the fields in Florida, I thought it was easy work. Having a loud voice helped; people used to tell me that they could hear me hollering ''Get your paper'' up on the fifteenth floors of the downtown office buildings.

But it gets awfully cold in Chicago during the winter, which is why my ears perked up when a guy in my neighborhood told me about his job setting pins at a local bowling center. He said that if I worked steadily from 5 p.m. to eight or nine, I could make three bucks or more a day. That was about a dollar a day more than I was making selling papers (two bucks a day apparently was the standard kid's wage in Chicago too back then), and I could stay warm besides. So I said ''sure.''

The lanes where I went to work—and got my initiation into bowling—were in the basement of a building at Ashland Avenue and Van Buren Street where the tailors' union had its headquarters. It was called the Amalgamated Center, I guess because ''amalgamated'' was part of the union's name. It was a clean little place, with six lanes for bowling, a couple of pool tables and a six-stool coffee counter. The union owned it, and a fellow named Joe Saviano was the manager. Tailors would use it after they were done working for the day.

I was 12 years old, so the year was 1945. That was before the automatic pinsetting machines that are everywhere these days. We pin boys would sit on a ledge in back of the lane, above where the balls would come in. After the bowler would roll, we'd pick up the pins, put them in a manual machine, pull the lever that set the pins back down in a triangle, and send the ball back along the track that was there for it. If you weren't used to heavy work, it could be pretty tiring, but with my farm-boy background it was strictly a piece of cake for me. Pretty soon I was setting two lanes at once, and on busy days when some of the other kids wouldn't show up, I'd handle three. Some days I'd earn four or five dollars, and I would pocket a dollar or two because I'd told my parents that the daily wage was three bucks. I liked that, and, being sportsminded, I also liked working in a place connected with a sport.

Kids being kids, we pin boys at the Amalgamated would try to turn our jobs into a game. We'd have contests to see who could set the racks fastest and send the balls back hardest so they'd hit the retaining rings on the bowlers' side with a "thwack." We'd do some daredevil stunts, too, like getting down from the ledges where we were supposed to sit and standing right in the pits when the balls would come in. If a bowler didn't throw too hard, you could sometimes field his ball before it hit the backstop, like a shortstop in softball. If you'd get hit with a flying pin, well, that was the price you paid for being a hero. I remember once sitting on my ledge drinking milk from a glass bottle, when a pin came flying up and smashed it. All that was left in my hand was the neck of the bottle, and milk and glass were everywhere. I was lucky that none of the glass got in my eyes.

It's natural that if you set pins in a bowling center, you bowl, too, and that's what I did. I remember that the first game I rolled was with a hard-cork ball—they stopped making them long ago—and I was in my stocking feet, because I didn't have bowling shoes. My first ball ever was a strike (hey!). My first full-game score was 75. That was enough to make me want to try again, and I got the hang of it pretty quickly after that.

Some of us pin boys would go to the Amalgamated right after school, at about 3:30 p.m., and set pins for one another until 4:30 or 5 o'clock, when the tailors would start arriving. Mr. Saviano would let us bowl free as long as we behaved ourselves. If I got to the center alone, I'd set up all six lanes in the place, go out front and bowl, and then run back and set them up again until it was time to start work.

A lot of the old-time bowling professionals started out as pin boys, just like a lot of the old-time golf pros began in their sport as caddies. I think I learned a few things about the game from watching from behind the pins, like the delivery techniques of different kinds of bowlers and the effects of various types of shots. It got so that I could just about tell by watching a ball's direction, speed and spin which pins it would knock down, and which it wouldn't. Sometimes, when I'm bowling, I still can shift my perspective so I can see the ball from the other side of the pins. I can't claim this gives me an edge over the fellows I play against today, almost all of whom grew up in the automatic-pinsetter era. But I think that being a pin boy gave me some insights into the game that I wouldn't have otherwise.

More was going on in my young life than pin-setting and

bowling, of course. I went to school and got good grades, mostly. I also played just about every sport you can name. I always was tall—I stood better than six feet when I entered high school—so I was good at basketball, and I could throw hard, which made me the pitcher on just about every kids' team on which I played. The big summer game for me and the other boys in our Near West Side neighborhood was 16-inch softball, which is popular only around Chicago and places where ex-Chicagoans live. It's played with a big ball and short bases, which lets it fit into the many parks around the city that are too small for baseball. Also, all you need to play is a ball and bat—no one wears a glove—so it's cheap. There were a lot of good athletes around the neighborhood, including a few who went into professional sports, but the biggest local hero was a fellow nicknamed "The Sheik" who played 16-inch softball in the Windy City League, which was the pinnacle of the sport. He pitched, and could hit 'em a mile. I could, too, relatively speaking, when I caught one right in a kids' game from my left-handed batting stance.

Another favorite pastime of the kids in the neighborhood wasn't a sport, it was fighting. It seemed like every block had its own gang, and if you looked cross-eyed at someone, you had a battle on your hands, although it was with fists or sticks, not knives and guns like the street gangs fight with today. My brothers and I had plenty of fights after we'd moved to Chicago to stay, because we were the "farmers" who didn't fit in. But we stood up for ourselves and one another, and eventually got accepted.

Most of the kids I ran with had goofy nicknames, like "Bootsy," "Dittie," "Goo-Goo," "Cocoa" and "Balloon Head," to name a few. I never had a nickname. I guess

"Carmen" was strange enough. My best budddy was "Naked Lou" Lenzi, who went on to play minor-league baseball. We called him "Naked Lou" because one night, when he'd snuck into a park swimming pool and stripped to go in the water, someone stole all his clothes, and he had to run home naked for about two blocks.

It was funny, though, because I was never as much of a hang-around kid as a lot of the others around where I lived. I always preferred to be with older guys than boys my own age, and play individual sports than team ones. I guess that's one reason I took to bowling. I know for sure the other reason: the fact that my parents insisted that I work after school ruled out my playing on the varsity teams at Crane Tech High. By combining bowling with pin-setting, I could play a sport and make a few dollars at the same time.

The more I bowled at the Amalgamated, the better I got. Just doing what came naturally, I got to be a steady 160-plus bowler by the time I was 14 years old. That was my age when I got into my first league, a handicap affair. All the other fellows on my team were grown men, working guys. We were sponsored by Delnero's, a produce business. They put me down for a 164-average to start, which was honest, but at that age I was improving practically by the week, and by the end of the season I was rolling over 180. Of course, my handicap in that league stayed at 36, the difference between 164 and 200, bowling's version of golf's "par." That was a big help for us in the standings. We took first place.

I still have some pictures someone took of that team. There I was, with lots of black hair, wearing baggy pants, an untucked shirt with a tee-shirt peeking through the collar, and old, scuffed bowling shoes that turned up at the toes.

They were rental shoes that Mr. Saviano from the Amalgamated gave me after they had pretty well worn out. They were the first bowling shoes I owned, and I appreciated them.

The only instruction I received was from a guy named Joe Ronosky, a tailor who bowled in the top league at the Amalgamated. He'd come early sometimes, watch me bowl, and make suggestions. We'd have discussions about how to hold the ball, and the approach and release. Ronosky used a two-hole ball, which was more common then than it is today. It gave him good control, but it meant that he couldn't put as much spin on the ball as it took to be a really top-flight bowler. He told me that, and recommended I stick with the three-hole ball. He had an old one around his home, and one day gave it to me as a gift. It was my first ball. I used it for years.

Ronosky's friendship was important to me for reasons other than bowling. I needed adult friendship because my father wasn't an easy man to get close to, and Ronosky provided that. He was a good person, someone I could talk with, and I appreciated his taking an interest in me. We bowled together some—he had about a 180-average—and I remember my feeling of accomplishment the first time I beat him. I later bowled in the same league he did, and took the prize for high average with a 198. I was 15 years old then. I got my trophy at a banquet after the season, and made a little speech thanking Joe for his help. He came up to shake my hand and give me a hug. That said it all about our relationship.

If it is possible to have a "career" as a pin boy, I had one. By the time I was 16 years old, and making a local reputation as a bowler, Schueneman & Flynn's, a bigger bowling center in the neighborhood, hired me away from the Amalgamated and made me a kind of chief pin-setter. It was my job to recruit pin boys and make out their work schedules. Later, when I'd saved enough money from my bowling hustling to buy a car, I'd go down to Skid Row and pick up rummies who would set pins nights after the school boys went home.

One old fellow who was a regular pin-setter at Schueneman & Flynn's used to be a physician, the head surgeon at a big Chicago hospital. He told me he became an alcoholic after his wife divorced him and took his children away. I only knew him as a drunk who sometimes wasn't sober even when he was setting pins, and that stuff about his previous life amazed me. With my limited background, I'd never known anyone like that. It opened my mind to the fact that all sorts of things were going on in the world that I hadn't heard about. I think that knowing old "Doc," and hearing him in his lucid periods talk about his previous life, started me toward becoming the student of human nature that I am today.

Schueneman & Flynn's was a real step up from the Amalgamated, class-wise. Bowling was really catching on in Chicago, and all over America, in the years just after World War II, and this center was a showplace. It had a fountain in the lobby and a restaurant where people could sit down for dinner in a suit and tie. Mr. Schueneman was an absentee owner, but his partner, Jim Flynn, who also was his son-in-law, used to come around the place. My bowling deal there was the same as it had been at Amalgamated. I'd come in after school with the other pin boys and bowl lines before the leagues started.

Jim Flynn heard about how good I was, and he showed up one afternoon to watch me. I bowled three or four games while he was there, and I don't think I scored under 210 in any of them. It blew his mind to think that a 16 year old could bowl like that. He became a fan of mine, and one of my biggest boosters.

Schueneman & Flynn's attracted more good bowlers than the tailor's union lanes—it was one of the hottest bowling centers in Chicago back then—and being there every day contributed a lot to my education. One of the most important things I learned was how to practice.

Now, most bowlers, including some very good ones, practice as though they were bowling in a league, rolling regular games with strikes and spares, and keeping score. I did that, too, of course, but I also learned that at bowling's top level, strikes are more important than spares, or, to put it better, getting lots of strikes in a row is what wins. Thus, I began devoting most of my practice time to honing my strike ball.

I also learned that keeping score is a waste of time and a needless diversion during practice. If you're scoring, you're looking at the numbers on the sheet, not at the pins, like you should. It's quite possible to bowl a decent score and still not be rolling the ball the way you should.

One afternoon, when I was bowling with the pin boys, I saw a guy crawling down one of the lanes at Schueneman & Flynn's on his hands and knees. I asked him what he was doing. "Looking at my lines," he said.

In those days, they polished the lanes with one of those circular buffers, like they use on waxed floors, and they'd just done that at S & F's. I got down on my knees with the guy, and I could see the ball-lines he was talking about. After that, I made it a point to bowl as often as I could just after the lanes had been buffed. I'd throw maybe 15 or 20 balls, and then lie flat on my belly to see the trails they left. If the lines were all over the place, I knew I was off and needed to work on getting a more consistent delivery. If the lines were the width of a half-dollar or less, I'd know I was on the right track.

With Jim Flynn's help, I got into the scratch league at Schueneman & Flynn's. Again, I was the only kid with a bunch of men. I bowled well, as usual—my average was over 200 by the time I was 17—and my reputation began to spread outside the neighborhood to the whole city. Angelo Biondi, the bowling writer for the *Chicago Daily News,* came out and interviewed me for an article. He wrote how I was the "boy wonder" of Chicago bowling, and a future champion.

All of a sudden, I was a celebrity. Before that story ran, my parents had only the foggiest notion about what I was doing besides setting pins at the bowling center at night. When their friends started congratulating them for having a famous son, they started taking more notice of me.

The publicity made people at Crane Tech High take notice, too. Guys I scarcely knew started buddying up to me, and teachers whom I didn't think knew I existed began asking me how things were going. I was always a good student in high school even though the lack of money around my house ruled out my going to college, but I usually was quiet in class. With everybody suddenly looking at me because of my new-found fame, I started talking up more.

I think it was partly because of my "boy wonder" publicity that Crane got together a bowling team during my junior and senior years. Jesse Beaver, a math teacher at the school and a 185-average bowler, volunteered to be the sponsor and coach. He and I got to be friendly, and later bowled doubles together in some tournaments. I was the first student at Crane who ever beat him, and I confess to taking him for a few dollars before he fully realized what was happening.

Mr. Beaver got up a league at the school because there were a lot of boys who bowled, and then he put together the best five players into an all-star team. Bowling wasn't a varsity sport in Chicago high schools then, but we booked matches against other schools anyway. And let me tell you, we had one heckuva team! I averaged 211 in my senior year, and my pal "Naked Lou" Lenzi had about a 190 average. I think our worst guy was about a 180 shooter. Our average for five guys was about 950 a game, which was better than a lot of the teams in the adult scratch leagues then.

Our team got some newspaper publicity, and that helped make me more famous. In my senior year at Crane, a city-wide high school tournament was put together at Pilsen Recreation on the South Side, with about 15 schools participating. Our team didn't win that one—I think we came in second or third—but I had the best individual score. The school was so proud that it gave us bowlers varsity letters even though ours wasn't a sanctioned high school sport.

I was 17 years old now, and bowling had become the biggest thing in my life. Just about every waking moment when I wasn't in school or sleeping, I was out bowling, either at S & F or the Amalgamated. I'd roll line after line, three or four hours every weekday, and 12 to 14 hours a day on weekends. Practice was a pleasure for me. I never got tired, and I never had to be persuaded to go. I don't bowl nearly that much now, but I still don't have to push myself to practice. When it stops being a pleasure, I'll quit.

Bowling and betting are linked inextricably for most people, and I was no exception. From the time I started fooling around afternoons with the other pin boys there was always a nickel or a dime on the games, and those sums mounted with my fame. I'll devote a later chapter to this side of bowling, but one incident that happened when I was a kid sticks particularly in my mind. I was 16 years old, and bowling at S & F, when a man came in. "I hear you're some kind of a hotshot. Want to shoot a few lines?" he said to me. Now, I didn't know this guy from Adam. He could have been Andy Varipapa in disguise. But I was young, and that hotshot line of his stung me. "Sure," I said. "For how much?"

He said he'd take it easy on me, and play me for a half-dollar a line. Cocky kid that I was, I told him to make it a dollar. That was very dumb of me, because all I had in my pocket was 25 cents.

Anyway, we started bowling, and the guy was good. We went five games and, luckily, I won three of them. Believe me, I sweat the whole time. I've since played for a lot more money than that buck a game, but I've never been more nervous. Playing for a dollar when you only have a quarter is my definition of pressure.

It was only a matter of time before I moved up in the bowling world, but the break came sooner than I expected. I was still in high school when I turned pro. The 1950 Illinois state tournament was being held at Schueneman & Flynn's, which by then was my home lanes, and I went to watch. All of the teams from the Chicago Classic League were there. It was the *creme de la creme* of bowling.

There are tough bowling centers just like there are tough golf courses, and S & F was among the toughest. Even the best bowlers had trouble recording good scores there. It almost always took a score of better than 3,000 to win a state team tournament, but the winning team that day shot 2,868.

Only one man, Bill Kenneth, averaged better than 200 for his nine games in all categories, and it won him the individual all-events championship.

The team that was on the bottom of the Classic League at the time was sponsored by the Alcazar Hotel. Its captain was Rudy Hazucha. He was about 40 years old, tall and square-built. He had a white-collar job, which was fairly unusual for professional bowlers then.

Hazucha wasn't a great bowler, but he was a good businessman and organizer, and it wasn't uncommon for that kind of fellow to captain a Classic League team. Alcazar being on the bottom and all, he was on the lookout for new talent. When some of the locals at S & F told him that a young kid was averaging 200 there, he demanded to be introduced. "Anybody who can average 200 in this place can do it anywhere on earth," he told me. "How about joining us?"

I was delighted, of course, but still being in high school (it was the spring of my senior year) it wasn't quite that easy. My parents had to give their permission first, and I told Hazucha to talk to them. He came out to our apartment, and it took him about a minute to get their approval. About all he had to say was that I'd be earning money bowling.

I figured I'd probably work my way into the Alcazar lineup during Classic League play the following season, and then move up to the national events, but that's not the way it turned out. The American Bowling Congress's (ABC) tournament, one of bowling's biggest annual championships, was scheduled for the week after I told Hazucha I'd join Alcazar. Before I'd even tried on the slacks and bowling shirts they gave me, I got a call that the wife of one of the team's members was going into labor with a new baby, and that I had to fill in.

The tournament ran from a Friday through a Monday, and I was supposed to be in school that week. But my folks signed a note to the principal that my brother, Joe, wrote, asking that I be excused, and the principal said okay. The Alcazar bowling uniforms were about the only really good clothes I had, so I packed them and some socks and underwear in a suitcase, along with my toothbrush, and went off to Union Station to join my teammates on the Santa Fe Railroad's Hiawatha train to St. Paul. At 17-1/2 years old, I was off to see the rest of the world.

2

Turning Pro

To say that I was nervous going into that first tournament in St. Paul would be an understatement: I was scared stiff. I mean, I'd bowled in some pretty fancy company around Chicago for a couple of years, and had some of those "boy wonder" stories about me in the newspapers. I'd also rolled more than a few games with real dollars on the line, by which I mean money that I put up myself. But this was the ABC Tournament, bowling's version of the World Series, and there I was, a 17-year-old kid, making his first appearance as an honest-to-goodness professional.

Me and the other guys from the Alcazar team stayed at a hotel near the tournament site that looked very grand to me. Johnny Giovanelli, one of my teammates, took me under his wing and made sure I had someone to eat with. He tried to help me take my mind off the tournament by taking me to the movies the night before we were to bowl, but it didn't work. I think if you'd have asked me what movie we'd seen five minutes after we'd left the theater, I couldn't have told you.

I wasn't any calmer once we got to the lanes. The tournament wasn't in a regular bowling center, but in an arena that they'd fixed up with temporary lanes just for the event. The place had a huge, high ceiling and seating all around for spectators. There must have been 4,000 or 5,000 people there, although at the time I probably would have guessed the number was 40,000 or 50,000. The lanes were elevated from the floor so you had to climb some stairs to get to them, and the lights were very bright and suspended from the ceiling rafters like theatrical spotlights. It felt more like going on stage than bowling.

My teammates on Alcazar that day were Rudy, Johnny, Les Kilbourne and Bill White. They had me bowling in the number-three slot, which meant that I wouldn't have the added pressure of leading off or finishing. I remember mounting the stairs to the lane and taking my ball off the rack, but, for the life of me, I can't recall a thing about that first ball I rolled. My next recollection is of going back to the bench, sitting down, and asking Johnny what happened. It was an almost-total blackout.

However that first ball turned out, I did okay afterward. I shot a 603 for three games in the team event and later that day had a respectable 578 in the doubles, where Kilbourne was my partner. A couple of days after that, in the singles, I popped a big 699 series, which stood up for fourth place. My prize was $1,000, by far the most money I'd ever won at anything. Under our team's rules, we split all prizes equally, so my take-home pay from that was just $200, but I was still on Cloud Nine about it. I came home to Schueneman & Flynn's and a hero's welcome. Jim Flynn didn't make me pay for lines for a month!

That summer, after I graduated from Crane Tech, I took a job doing stock work at Alden's, a mail order house. That was typical of professional bowlers at the time. Very few guys could earn enough money from the sport to support themselves, so most had jobs as well. They were bakers, policemen or salesmen, or ran bowling-supply stores, and bowled on evenings and weekends. It would be many years before the prizes became large enough to make the sport a full-time proposition for a sizable number of top players.

Of course, while I was stacking boxes at Alden's, I was dreaming about bowling in the Chicago Classic League. I'd bowled in the ABC tournament with Alcazar, but never in league play. And league play was where it was at for most of the pros for most of the years during the 1950s, just as it had been for a couple of decades before.

The reason that the leagues dominated was that they alone could attract sponsor money. Companies could get a ton of newspaper publicity by backing teams in the "Classic" or "Major" Leagues that flourished in Chicago, St. Louis, Detroit, Cleveland, Milwaukee, and some of the other big bowling cities back then. It didn't cost them much, either. Although deals varied from city to city, team to team, and even player to player, the big majority of the pros received no salaries from the teams for which they bowled. The sponsors put up uniforms and equipment, and some traveling expenses. They also paid their bowlers' entry fees for some tournaments, including the ABC. But that was about all they put up. The bowlers on a team usually shared the prize money they won, either as a group or individually. Everything went into a pot that the guys split, one-fifth share for everybody, at the end of the season. Whenever a team or team member won anything his sponsor's name was mentioned, and twice every week from fall through spring, when the Classic League rolled, the sponsor would see its name in the scores and standings that the newspapers carried the next day.

As any league bowler will confirm, there are some nice things about being a member of a team. Team bowling has a social side that individual-tournament bowling lacks, and you get to know some interesting people that way. Being a member of a half-dozen Chicago Classic League teams over a 10-year period allowed me to meet some of the sport's greatest names. Every city thought that its own Classic League was the best back then, but if they were fair-minded, even die-hard Detroiters or St. Louisans would agree that Chicago had a lot going for it in the early 1950s.

I mean, we are talking about guys who were the bowling gods of the period: Buddy Bomar, Ned Day, Paul Krumske, Joe Norris, Junie McMahon and Joe Wilman, to name a few. They're all in the ABC Hall of Fame now. I bowled with or against all of them, starting at age 17. My experience, I guess, is what it might have been like to have played baseball with Joe Di Maggio, Mickey Mantle, Hank Aaron and Willie Mays, and still be an active professional ballplayer today.

I think that if you had asked an average sports fan in the late 1940s or early 1950s to name a single bowler, he would have picked Buddy Bomar. Bomar wasn't the best bowler of the period; Don Carter or Ned Day were. Bomar, however, with his square jaw, ever-ready smile and neatly combed black hair, was the game's leading personality.

Bomar was an operator first and a bowler second, although, as his 1945 Bowler of the Year Award showed, he was outstanding on the lanes. He had a gift of gab that enabled him to talk his sponsors out of the top dollar, which meant that his teams always traveled first-class. It also meant that he could recruit top bowlers from all over the country. Ned Day came from Milwaukee to play with him in Chicago, as did Eddie Kawolics from Cleveland and Joe Kristof from Toledo. He recruited me for his Munsingwear team in 1955.

Bomar always was a fellow to play the angles, and the stunts he pulled on behalf of his teams would fill a book the size of this one. His best trick came in the late 1940s, when his and Day's Tavern Pale team bowled the E & B's from Detroit for the national team championship. In those days many of the major titles, individual as well as team, were fought out on a home-and-home basis, with each team bowling once on its home lanes and then traveling to the other guy's place. Total pins decided the trophy.

Bomar's home lanes was Samuelson's Bowl on the North Side of Chicago, and he decided he'd take full advantage of it this time. Lanes then were coated with shellac, which got very hard when the temperature dropped. For a couple of wintery nights before the match, Bomar opened all the windows in the place so that the shellac got like ice, and then he'd buff the lanes to make them slicker still. He had his team out practicing in sweaters and scarves so they could handle those conditions. On match day, he didn't turn on the heat at Samuelson's until the last minute—too late for the lanes to "thaw"—and he had his buffers out again. Needless to say, his team won, and after that Bomar's nickname among the bowlers was "Buffy."

Ned Day was a quite-different sort, a man who was always quiet and gentlemanly. His greatest days as a bowler were in the early 1940s, when he twice won Bowler of the Year honors, but he still was a formidable guy when I came up. He was a short fellow, standing only five-feet-seven or eight inches tall, and was very fussy about his appearance. His hair was so perfectly waved you would swear he had it set. If you went to shake hands with him, he'd wrap a towel around his fingers to protect them, and give you a very soft grip.

Day bowled pretty much the same way he looked. His delivery was as smooth as I've ever seen, and he had great repetition, by which I mean that he could throw the same shots over and over again. When he released a ball, you'd never hear a bang or a bump, just a soft hum. He was the picture of what a bowler should be.

The guy I remember most vividly was Paul Krumske. There was a character. He was about five-feet-eight inches tall, and skinny to boot, but he was one of the fiercest competitors I've ever come across. He'd run over his grandma to win a match, and if you got in his way, he'd try to run over you, too.

I bowled against Krumske, and with him on the Meister Brau teams that won a couple of Chicago Classic League titles. Believe me, I'd much rather bowl with him than against him, if only because he was one of the most fidgety bowlers who ever lived. He had this habit of rubbing his right hand up and down his pant leg before he threw. He did it so often he would drive people crazy, spectators as well as opponents. Once, in a match against Day, he needed a strike to clinch in the tenth frame, and he stood there for minutes on end, rubbing that hand on his pants. A lady in the crowd couldn't take it any more. "...thirty-four...thirty-five...thirty-six," she counted. "Throw the ball already!" Krumske stopped, gave her a dirty look, and started rubbing all over again. He threw when he was good and ready—and got his strike. "Lady, that was for you," he said after the pins dropped.

Krumske would go to great lengths to put an opponent off his game. He had a heart condition—or, at least, he always said he did—and a couple of times he faked heart attacks to upset his foes. Once, he stopped in the middle of a match game he was losing to Day, went into the men's room, and started groaning like he was going to die. Poor Ned, gentle soul that he was, became so upset that when the match resumed his strikes became few and far between.

Another time, when his Meister Brau's were getting beat by the tough Pfeiffer beer team out of Detroit, Krumske poked his teammates and whispered, "No matter what I do, don't let it bother you." With that he stood up, grabbed his chest, and collapsed on a lane approach. An ambulance was called and 15 or 20 minutes elapsed before it arrived while the Pfeiffer's stood around getting cold and confused. By the time the medics showed up, Krumske was sitting up and saying how he felt much better. They gave him a little oxygen and he jumped to his feet and started throwing strikes. His teammates followed suit. He'd turned the match.

I had a run-in with Paul in a league at the old Uptown Melody Lanes in Chicago. In those days, there was no electric eye to detect fouls, and it was up to an official to call them. We were bowling for different teams in adjacent lanes, and he claimed I fouled. I said I didn't, and the official backed me up. That got him so angry that he wanted to fight me. Here was this skinny, little guy, jumping up and down (no sign of a heart condition here!) and threatening to flatten someone who was six inches taller and outweighed him by 40 pounds. First I got mad back, but when I realized how silly the whole thing looked I started to laugh. The guys who jumped in to separate us began laughing, too, and, pretty soon, so did Krumske. We shook hands and went about our business.

The next year Paul recruited me for his Meister Brau team, and I got an every-day look at how good he was. If my life was on the line, and my team needed three strikes in the tenth frame to win a game, he was one of three guys I'd choose to get them. The other two would be Junie McMahon, a star of the late 1940s and early 1950s whose career probably was shorter than it should have been because of a drinking problem, and Dick Weber, the dominant bowler of the late 1960s, who some say was the best ever.

Krumske was so good that I'd swear he'd bowl poorly sometimes just so he could make a dramatic comeback. Once, in a team match, I got mad at him after he had fooled around for nine frames and then struck out in the tenth to give us a one-pin win. "If you'd have bowled better before, you would have saved us a lot of stress and strain," I said. Krumske gave me a disgusted look. "Damnit kid, we won, didn't we?" he snapped. "You don't appreciate nothin'."

If Paul Krumske exemplified the competitive side of team bowling, Joe Norris represented its lighter side. He was in his middle 40s by the time I became his teammate on the Tri Par Radio team that won the ABC team title in 1954, but he still had a lot of good bowling—and good times— left in him.

Norris was always up to some kind of trick. He'd stuff cotton in the holes of your ball so your fingers wouldn't fit right, or hide your street shoes while you were on the lanes. I'm a sound sleeper, and several times I woke up in my hotel room on the road to find my pants hanging from a light fixture or my underwear out on a window ledge, courtesy of good old Joe.

I remember once, during the summer, Tri Par was supposed to bowl in the Ray Schalk Tournament on the South Side of Chicago. Joe lived in the same neighborhood as the bowling center and invited us over for lunch before we were supposed to go on. I was a big 7-Up drinker at the time, and Norris knew it. When I got to his house I told him I was thirsty, and he told me to go to the refrigerator and help myself. I opened the door and there were six green 7-Up bottles. I took one, opened it, and started gulping. I must have had the thing half empty before I discovered I was drinking white vinegar, not 7-Up! The first thing I grabbed for was my throat, and the second was for Norris's throat. He's laughing and yelling, "I'm a teammate! I'm a teammate!" while the other guys were pulling us apart.

When things quieted down, and I had a chance to think over what had happened (and chase the vinegar taste), it occurred to me that Norris had lucked out on his joke because I'd probably picked the only 7-Up bottle in his fridge that he'd filled with vinegar. I told him my theory, and he had another laugh at my expense. "I filled up all six for you!" he roared.

As every league bowler knows, team bowling has a dynamic all its own. When we'd put our Classic League teams together, we'd usually lead off with a "rah-rah" guy, somebody with a lot of spirit who could get the other fellows stirred up. Norris was perfect for this spot. Your No. 2 man would be the fourth-best bowler of your five starters, and your No. 3 would be the weakest. The object was to tuck those fellows safely away from the pressures that would emerge in the late stages of tough matches, although in the ''major'' leagues they were always solid bowlers. The No. 4 man would be a steady guy who could always be counted on to ''mark''— that is, get a strike or spare—in a frame. A lot of times he'd have the best overall average on the squad. The No. 5, or anchor, bowler would be the one most likely to come through in the clutch, whether or not he had the best average on the team. Krumske almost always bowled anchor on his teams, for instance.

There was a lot of by-play in league bowling, and not a little gamesmanship. Bomar was an accomplished needler; he had a knack of getting an opponent's goat but without getting the guy so mad he'd resort to violence. Buzz Fazio also was in that category; in fact, all things considered, I'd rank Buzz as the best *team* man I ever came across. He was an excellent individual bowler, of course, but there was something about the team situation that brought out the best in him.

Buzz had a lot of Buddy Bomar's brand of larceny in him, too. In the days of the short-lived National Bowling League, my Dallas team went to Omaha to bowl Buzz's team. He had a bunch of straight-ball bowlers, so he laid strips of masking tape from the right sides of the foul lines to the pockets and then had the lanes oiled heavily. His boys could use that dry strip like a track, while the hookers on my team were sliding all over the place. It wasn't against the rules, so all we could do was complain.

I bowled with some great teams in my day, but though I enjoyed team bowling, I always thought of myself as an individual bowler first and a team guy second. I like action, and I'd get antsy waiting around for my turn to bowl in a five-man league rotation. Also, I'm afraid, I had a short-fuse temper during the days when professional team bowling was at its height.

I got into a lot of scrapes as a younger fellow, but the one that comes to mind quickest involved Fazio. His Falstaff team out of St. Louis was bowling Krumske's and my Meister Braus for the national team title in 1957. During the warmups in the Chicago segment of the home-and-home series (which, incidentally, the Falstaffs were to win), Fazio heckled me from the bench. When that didn't get the rise he wanted, he tossed a towel under my feet on my approach.

I rolled that ball calmly enough, but on my next trip I released my ball backwards, towards the bench where Buzz was sitting. He went for me, and everybody jumped up and pulled us apart. It was a good ten minutes before things calmed down to where we could bowl again.

I was wrong to do what I did because I could have cracked a rack of Buzz's ribs if I'd hit him with the ball. In that case, I guess, Buzz would have been within his rights to call the police and sock me with a fat hospital bill. But, of course, I didn't think of that at the time.

As I look back on things from the perspective of middle age, I realize I wasn't always the best-behaved kid when I first turned pro. In fact, I think I can say without fear of contradiction that I was arrogant and mouthy, and that I had a chip on my shoulder the size of a log. None of those characteristics made me easy to like.

In my defense, I must say that I had some excuses. One was that I met with quite a bit of hostility from some of the established bowlers when I first came out of Schueneman & Flynn's to become the youngest bowler in the Chicago Classic League, especially from some of the more marginal players. They resented the attention I was getting, and were afraid that I was going to take the bread out of their mouths.

One guy I had a problem with early was, of all people, Rudy Hazucha, my captain on the Alcazar Hotel team. I joined the team in regular league play the autumn after my 699 series got me that fourth-place national finish in the 1951 ABC tournament in St. Paul, and I picked up right where I'd left off. The first 10 weeks of the season I rolled consecutive 600-plus series, and led the league with a 209 average.

Hazucha, however, told me that I wasn't the bowler I should be, and that I'd be better if I copied his style. His style couldn't have been more different from mine. He lined up on the far right side of the lane and threw a straight ball. I lined up towards the left and threw a huge hook. But I was a kid and he was the captain, so it was his way or the highway.

I don't have to tell you what happened. I did what he told me for a couple of weeks and bowled 180s instead of 210s. We didn't have the greatest team to begin with, and the experiment just made us worse. He finally gave up and let me go back to throwing the ball my own way. But by then I was pretty sour on the whole situation, and was determined to switch teams at my earliest opportunity.

The incident that really set my style for my first half-dozen years as a pro—for better or worse—took place at one of my first important tournaments. That was the 1951 City Match Game Championships in Chicago. The Match Game was a round-robin affair in which not only total pins counted but also whether or not you beat the men you were pitted against. To the suprise of many, including me, I led after the first few rounds of play.

I remember coming home from the tournament feeling

really good. The family sat down to dinner, and my brother
Joe, who had gone to watch me bowl that day, mentioned
that one of the bowlers—he said he couldn't remember
who—had told him that I wasn't respectful to the older guys
I was facing. Joe said it in a kidding manner, as if to ask,
''Aren't those guys ridiculous?'' But my father and mother
didn't take it as a joke and neither did I. I left the table, so
upset I couldn't eat, and the feeling didn't leave me for the
rest of the tournament. I dropped from first place all the way
to twelfth, one place shy of qualifying for the All-Star
Tournament, one of the biggest events on the year's calendar.

My first thought was that whoever made that remark was
being terribly unfair to me, because I was, too, ''respectful''
to the older fellows. The more I thought about it, though,
the madder I became. What right did another bowler have
to expect respect from me just because I was younger? We
were all competitors together, trying to win, and winning
was the name of the game as long as you followed the rules.
I vowed to go my own way, and to hell with anybody who
didn't like it. I made up my mind to never let what somebody
said bother me. And while I didn't always keep that pledge,
I sure developed a much tougher skin than I'd had before.

You have to understand that I was no shrinking violet
before the ''no respect'' incident. My first taste of publicity
caught me by surprise, but I have to admit that the more I
read about myself, the more I liked it. Muhammad Ali wasn't
the first professional athlete to realize that getting his name
before the public, even in an off-beat way, could pay dividends. I was pulling publicity stunts long before he came
along. And, I suppose, like Ali's stunts, mine didn't always
make everybody love me.

My best gimmick, which has stuck with me for my entire

career, wasn't my own idea, but Joe Wilman's. Joe was my teammate on Tri Par Radio in 1954, and someone who always got my respect through the simple method of deserving it. A nicer man never rolled a bowling ball, and few rolled one better. He was the All-Star champion in 1945 and Bowler of the Year in 1946. One of the things I'm proudest about in bowling was that I helped him win the BPAA doubles in 1952. More about that later.

Wilman returned my affection, becoming a sort of father figure for me, although sometimes he was my henchman as well. He gave me the nickname "Spook," for no other reason than that he thought I was jumpy, or "spooky." He put Joe Norris up to buying and giving me an ink pad and stamp with one of those big-nosed "Kilroy Was Here" figures that you saw everywhere after World War II (as my picture shows, my real nose isn't exactly small). It had the caption "Spook Was Here" printed under it.

Well, that was all I needed. I took the "Spook" stamp and began stamping everything I could reach. I'd put the thing on every score sheet in a bowling center, and after the place had closed I'd sneak into the rest rooms and unroll, stamp and re-roll the toilet paper. I'd stamp people's skin with it when they weren't looking, and a few women had me stamp their bras. Walls, ceilings, floors, mirrors—the stamp went everywhere.

Pretty soon, "Spook" became my nickname, even among people who'd never seen the stamp. The newspapers picked it up, too, which was okay with me because it gave me some notice and was preferable to some of the other things I was being called. And I have to admit that the name was justified because of some of the spooky stunts I pulled over the years.

I guess the episode that the bowlers remember most happened in Houston, Texas, during a trip I took with the Meister Brau team when I was 23 or 24 years old. Some of us were sitting in the coffee shop at the Shamrock Hotel, looking out at the huge pool. The diving board caught the eye of Chuck Hamilton, one of my teammates. "Man, that is *high*," he exclaimed.

I was sitting back a way and couldn't see the whole pool, but I didn't let that stop me from jumping right in, to the conversation, that is. "Ah, that's not so high," I said. "I dived off higher boards every summer in the Chicago park pools when I was a kid."

"You couldn't dive off the high dive here," said Hamilton.

"I sure could, but I don't have a bathing suit," I replied.

With that, Hamilton got up and left the table. Next thing I knew, he was back with a bathing suit and a $20 bill. "Here's a suit," he said. "The twenty dollars says you'll chicken out."

Naturally, I couldn't pass up a challenge like that, so I took the suit and went into the men's room to put it on. It was too tight, which made me feel stupid, but I managed to squirm into it. I went out to the pool, climbed to the diving platform, and executed a neat swan. I returned to claim my twenty bucks and well-deserved applause.

Instead, there was Hamilton, grinning. "What was that, a warmup?" he asked. "That wasn't the board I was talking about. I meant the one up there."

He pointed to a part of the pool I hadn't seen from where I'd been sitting. That board looked more than twice as high as the one I'd dived from. Professional divers used it in shows they put on at the hotel. My eyes bugged, and I hoped no one noticed.

So out again I went. I got to the base of that high dive

and looked up. It looked 50 stories tall. "When you get to the top, you'd better keep moving," I told myself. "If you stop even for a second, they'll have to call the fire department to get you down."

I climbed the stairs, marched to the end of the platform, and let go. My dive turned into a half-belly-flop, which was fortunate because otherwise I might have hit bottom. I kid you not, I was black and blue all over my chest and stomach when I got out of the water, and I ached for a month.

My rewards included my buddies' respect along with the $20. "Carmen, if we ever need a strike from you in the tenth frame and you don't get it, I'll know one thing for sure: You didn't choke," said Hamilton.

Of course, no amount of craziness could make a star out of me if I couldn't bowl. But I could—and how! I don't think anyone ever made as big a splash as a pro as young as I did. I got my fourth place in the ABC singles at the age of 17. At 18, in 1952, I won my first major tournament, the Dom DeVito Classic.

"The Dom," as we called it, isn't around now, but it was big stuff in those days. DeVito, the man it was named after, was a star with the Duffy Florals team of Chicago that won a string of national titles in the 1920s. Hank Marino, the greatest bowler of that era, also was a member of that team. Joe Norris, my teammate at Tri Par Radio, was a youngster on the Detroit Palace squad that defeated Duffy Florals in the 1929 team finals and ended their reign.

The 1952 Dom DeVito was held at Chatham Bowl on the South Side of Chicago and drew a field of about 3,000 entrants. I bowled on the first day of the tournament, which was to go on for about three months. I'd bowled in a league the night before, and afterwards went to the Marigold Bowl on the North Side to roll a few match games with some friends. One thing led to another, and we kept at it until eleven o'clock the next morning. I went home, got a few hours of sleep, and was bright eyed and bushy tailed for a 6 p.m. start at Chatham. When you're 18 years old, you can get away with stuff like that.

I knew from my first practice ball that the tournament would be a tough one. The pins behaved like they were filled with lead, and they might have been. Someone told me they weighed three pounds, twelve ounces, which is about as heavy as they ever made them. Pins in professional tournaments in the 1970s and 1980s got as light as three pounds, two ounces before the ABC stepped in and set a three-pound, six-ounce minimum. You almost never see pins that weigh three pounds, 12 ounces anymore.

I did the best I could, and got a 1,661 score for eight games, or an average of just over 207. You wouldn't think that would hold up against a field that included just about every big name in the Midwest, but it did. My first-place check was for $3,000, which I split the usual five ways with the other guys on the Alcazar Hotel team. I also got a ton of publicity for being the youngest guy ever to win such an important tournament. It didn't hurt at all that, by bowling in the tournament's first squad, my name was in the newspapers at the top of tournament standings every day for the three months the thing ran.

My next big win came the same year in the BPAA national doubles, with Wilman. It was funny how we got together for that one. Usually, the sponsors preferred that you bowl the doubles tournaments with a guy from your own team, but the other fellows on Tri Par Radio had paired off, leaving Joe the odd man out, and Alcazar hadn't planned to send anyone because we hadn't done well in the Classic League and didn't have much money to spare. But Joe wanted to go to the tournament, and knew and liked me from league play, so he approached Rudy Hazucha and asked if Alcazar would send just me. I'd led the team in average for the season, and Rudy finally said that I could go, as a sort of reward.

Joe and I were about as unusual a pair as ever won a big doubles tourney. Joe was 47 years old and thought by some to be washed up as a top-flight bowler. He was a mild-mannered guy whose nickname was "Black Jack" because he liked to chew that awful, licorice-flavored gum of the same name. He threw a soft, slow ball, but was a master strategist, able to adapt his game to any set of lanes. I, of course, was a brash kid of 18 going on 19, with a big, powerful hook.

We almost didn't make it to St. Paul, where the qualifying rounds were held. We had planned to go on the same train, with me leaving from Union Station in Chicago and Joe, who lived in the western suburbs, picking it up in LaGrange, Illinois. Trouble was, that train didn't stop in LaGrange. I remember looking out the window as we flashed by, watching poor Joe standing there with his suitcase and bowling-bag on the platform. I didn't know whether to laugh or cry.

Joe caught a plane the next day and just made it in time to Harkins Lanes, where the tournament was held. He was all discombobulated from the hurry-up trip, and wasn't bowling well to start. The veteran George Young from Detroit was in our foursome, and needled Joe about it. "Good thing you got this kid to carry you," he said, pointing to me. That was all Joe needed to hear. He averaged 240 for the next six games, and we finished in second place, behind the team of Don Carter and Fred Bujack. Carter was the best bowler around then, and Bujack was no slouch, either. Both later were elected to the ABC Hall of Fame.

In those days, the second-place finishers in the BPAA national qualifiers could challenge whoever finished first to a home-and-home series for the championship. Challenges weren't automatic, because some expense was involved and you had to depend on ticket sales to make it worth your while financially. But Carter, Bujack and Wilman were big attractions, and I was getting to be one, so we took a shot and threw down the gauntlet.

Carter and Bujack got the home edge first, and beat us by 248 pins in a 24-game weekend set in Detroit. Then it was our turn to pick the lanes, and Wilman did a smart thing. "We'll bowl wherever you feel most comfortable," he told me. "I'll figure out a way to adapt."

I naturally picked my old stomping grounds of Schueneman & Flynn's. No one in the world could beat me there, I thought. Not only was it my home, but, like I've said before, outsiders always had a terrible time scoring well.

Just about everybody from my neighborhood was there to root for Joe and me. I don't think I ever bowled before a noisier, friendlier crowd. Carter and Bujack acted like one of those American Davis Cup tennis teams that winds up playing somewhere like Paraguay. We whipped 'em by 650 over the last 24 games, and took the crown. I averaged 206 for the 48 games, and Joe averaged 198. Carter and Bujack came in at 190 and 185, respectively.

My partnership with Wilman in the 1952 doubles led to my joining Tri Par Radio in time for the 1954 ABCs in Seattle, Washington. I'm not sure whether it was the best team I ever bowled on. The Meister Braus, with Paul Krumske, Ed Kawolics, Earl Johnson, Chuck Hamilton and Harry

Lippe, might have had more firepower. But it was plenty good enough.

Joe Norris was the lead-off man for Tri Par in the '54 ABCs and, like I've said, he was one of the best ever in that spot. Chuck Wagner and Harry Ledene, Jr., a couple of solid pros, bowled Nos. 2 and 3. I was No. 4, and Wilman bowled anchor. Art Butler was the captain, but he sat out the tournament. He was another one of those fellows whose main skill was for organizing.

We took to the lanes in the Seattle Coliseum in an evening session near the end of the tournament. I always preferred to bowl closer to the beginning of tournaments than to the end because I thought it was easier just to go out and do your best rather than try to beat a standing score. But that night, before a good-sized crowd that came to root for the two "Old Joes," everything came up golden. My 698 series led a three-game score of 3,226, which won the title for Tri Par. I also did well enough in the singles and doubles to finish third in the all-events division at the tournament.

My other big win in 1954 came in the Chicago Match Game Championships, and it was very special for me. This was a tournament in which the top 25 qualifiers met in a round-robin series of matches that took place over a couple of weekends. Rivalries that percolated all through the Classic League season came to a head in this one. It's one thing to go into a medal-play tourney like the Dom DeVito, roll a six-game block, and then go home and read the newspapers about what your competitors are doing, and quite another to go head-to-head against everybody who was anybody in Chicago bowling. An extra incentive for me was that the Match Game was the scene of the "no respect" episode that had upset me so much three years before. I was out to show that I couldn't be put off my game that easily again.

I got an edge in this tournament because of a format change that favored me. Before, you'd bowl a two-game set against an opponent on a pair of lanes, but that year they put each match on a single lane. As a young bowler, I wasn't as swift to adapt to different lanes as I later became, and a second game on the same surface allowed me to zero-in my hook. In one early-round match against Joe Norris, I went from a 193 first-game score to a 279 in the second. Norris said right there that the tournament was made for me to win, and that's the way it turned out. I won 20 of 24 matches against a field that included Norris, Wilman, Bomar, Krumske, Kawolics, Lippe and the rest of the Classic League's who's who. Facing down those guys one at a time meant more to me than the check I cashed for winning. In fact, now that I think of it, I can't remember how much money I won in that one.

I had just turned 21 years of age, which meant that I finally was eligible to vote and drink. As a bowler, though, I'd already won more major titles than some pros do in a lifetime.

"You're a noisy kid, but you're a talented one," Joe Wilman liked to say to me. He was right on both counts.

3

Fast Carmen

Being good didn't make me rich or even nearly rich, however; things didn't work that way in bowling in the early 1950s, or for a good twenty years thereafter. As I've said before, few professional bowlers could make a living competing for the prizes that were offered in those pre-television and pre-PBA days. Some fellows—and I was one of them for a time—supplemented their tournament incomes by giving lessons, but individual instruction of the kind that has long supported most golf pros never caught on in bowling. So most of the guys had salaried jobs or spent their nine-to-fives standing behind the counters in their bowling-equipment stores.

Or . . . they hustled. Which is to say that they bowled against other people. For money.

Now, I know what you're thinking: that "hustling" means cheating. You probably remember the movie *The Hustler,* where a

pool shark played by Paul Newman travels around and pre-
tends to be a lousy player until he suckers some unsuspect-
ing citizen into making an unwise wager. Hey! That was a
great movie, and I loved it, too. But that wasn't always how
things really were.

I'm proud to say that I hustled plenty when I was getting
started in the game, and won a lot of money. In fact, the
bulk of my income for my first half-dozen years as a bowling
professional came from wagering. But I never cheated, or
pretended to be anything I wasn't.

A few guys did do that. I remember a fellow out of Dallas
named Bob Prince. He would go into a center in a town,
bowl eight or 10 lines and shoot, maybe, 160 a game. What's
more (and far more difficult), he would *look* like a 160
bowler. Then he would entice some average bowler into a
betting game and just manage to edge him out.

I never used that approach, partly because I didn't want
to waste time—and possibly wreck my game—by pretending
to be ordinary, and partly because it didn't fit my personality.
I was more like John L. Sullivan or Muhammad Ali, the
boxers. I'd go into a place, proclaim that I was the greatest,
and offer to bowl any man in the house for whatever stakes
he named. You might be surprised at how many people took
me up on that, and for how long.

My main ally was the undisputable fact that bowling is
a gambling game for almost everyone who plays it. Whenever
you see two or more people bowling together, whether it's
in a league or just to pass the time, you can bet that there's
a bet involved. I don't know why that is; it just is. It's the
same with golf, pool, shuffleboard, or a lot of other one-
against-one games. I suppose that people just like to gamble.

To show how far some average-guy bowlers like to take

the betting thing, let me tell you about a bunch of fellows who have a team in a neighborhood near where I live. Every Wednesday night for the last 25 years, they've bowled in a church men's league. Rarely does a ball go down a lane without some cash riding on it.

For instance, every time a member misses the head pin with his first ball, he has to put a dime into the team kitty. Every time someone doesn't strike or spare in a frame, it costs him 20 cents, and if he's "open" in the last frame, it's 30 cents. If someone knocks down fewer than five pins on his first ball after a spare, he's fined a dime.

Any gutter ball costs one dollar. Whoever gets the low number of pins in the beer frame, the fifth, also kicks in a buck. If a fellow's total score is lower than his season's average, it costs him 25 cents.

If one man on the team gets a double—two strikes in a row—the other guys have to pay 25 cents each. Each strike over two straight costs them a dime more. If four team members strike in a frame, the guy who doesn't strike has to pay one dollar. If three guys strike, the two who didn't pay a quarter each. I think the list goes on, but those are all the items I remember.

At the end of the season, the guys split the kitty five ways, even-steven. They tell me it usually comes to between $200 and $300 each. It's not just the winning or losing that counts, because none of the guys keeps exact track of how much he contributes over the course of a season. It's the added edge—the excitement—that having a few dollars riding on their games gives them.

I have to confess that I'm an action guy, too, and that the money side of bowling has always turned me on. But maybe not in the way that you might think. It wasn't the money that mattered to me most, but the winning. I always wanted to beat the other guy, and let him and anybody else within shouting distance know that I beat him. Usually, the more money that rode on a game, the bigger was the crowd that gathered, and the more celebrity that went with winning. When I was a kid especially, but even now, fame was the name of the game for me, once the rent and grocery bills were paid, of course.

In the beginning, though, I bet so that I could bowl. In my pin boy days, the people at the Amalgamated and Schueneman & Flynn's let us kids bowl a few lines free before we went to work, but it wasn't long before I was bowling after work, too. Having to turn nearly all my earnings over to my parents meant that I didn't have much money to pay for lines. I let the boys I bowled with pay by taking them for line money.

That was harder than it might seem. From the first month or so I was better than the kids I bowled with, and, of course, they knew it. These were not dumb guys, and there was no way they were going to let me put my hand in their pockets without a little footwork. So I thought up gimmick bets, like bowling them left-handed (I'm a natural righty), releasing my ball flat-footed from the foul line without an approach, or rolling the ball towards the pins backwards, between my legs. I'm not bragging when I say that I'm such a superior athlete that I usually was able to come out ahead even with handicaps like those. And my buddies got such a kick out of seeing me do those stunts that they didn't much seem to mind my taking their dimes and quarters.

I had just turned 16 years of age when I had my first match for important money. My opponent was ''Lefty'' Masera; I don't think I ever knew his real name. Lefty was about 25 years old and lived in my neighborhood. I remember that he was tall, dark-haired, good-looking—kind of like me. He was a nice fellow and a real good bowler. When my reputation as a kid phenom bumped into his as the top gun, bowling-wise, of the Near West Side of Chicago (or, at least the Italian part of it), a meeting became inevitable.

The match was set up for $100 on a home-and-home basis. My $100 was put up by the little group of buddies and followers I had collected. I think that only about $20 of it was mine, but that was plenty because it was just about all the cash I had. I don't know where Lefty got his money. Maybe it was all his, because he had some kind of regular job.

We'd agreed to roll the first block of six games at Schueneman & Flynn's. Naturally, word about the match got around, and it attracted a pretty big crowd, mostly pro-me. I was as comfortable at S & F as I was in my own living room, and I whipped Lefty good there.

Then it was my turn to go to his place, which was G & L Bowl at Chicago and Crawford Avenues, a few miles west of S & F's. I showed up with my retinue of eight or 10 guys to find maybe 150 people, all fans of Lefty's, waiting for the match to start. The proprietor of the place had closed off the lanes on either side of the ones on which we were to bowl, and set up bleachers. It was like the Los Angeles Lakers coming into Boston Garden to play the Celtics in the seventh game of a National Basketball Association championship series.

I was rattled pretty good, and lost the first three games of the six-game set by a sizeable margin. Lefty's people started hollering things like "Where's the boy wonder?" and "When are you gonna start to bowl, Salvino?" I wish I could say that I went out and knocked their eyes out with a 300 game, but I can't because I didn't. I did improve enough to about break even over the last three games, though. And that, with the big lead I'd come in with, was enough to win. I went home $20 richer and a lot wiser.

After that, while still in high school, I routinely bowled adults for stakes of $10 to more than $100, winning a whole lot more than I lost. I let my mother in on what I was doing, and she agreed to serve as my banker, saving my winnings and giving me what I needed to stay in action. In return, I let her keep $10 a week, which was twice what I'd been giving her from my pin-setting jobs. As far as I know, she only told Dad about the $10-a-week part of the deal, because gambling was definitely not to his tastes. I did such a good job of winning, and Mom did such a good job of saving, that I was able to buy myself a car in less than a year. Having wheels vastly increased my hustling range.

I also picked up a manager of sorts: my older brother, Joe. He knew a good thing when he saw one, and he saw one in me. On nights and weekends, when he wasn't working, we'd get in my car and head for a bowling center in the sub-urbs or a city neighborhood where I wasn't known. I'd get on the lanes and bowl a few games for line money with the locals. He'd go through the crowd of onlookers, offering to bet on "the kid." He was shorter than me, and always dressed neatly while I was kind of sloppy, so people wouldn't put us together as brothers. When he'd get $15 or $20 dollars' worth of action on a game, he'd give me a wink, and I'd know that a bet was on. I never held back, and pretty soon I'd be wiping out everyone in the place. Instead of scaring people away, that only seemed to whet their appetites for more. It would be nothing for Joe and me to clear $150 to $200 in a weekend.

I had three things going for me as a hustler besides my bowling skill. One was my youth; people simply refused to believe that anyone as young as I was could bowl as well as I could. Another was my big mouth. I'd goad the guys I'd bowl against, telling them that I was going to whip their asses, and rubbing it in after I'd done it. "What's the matter with you, getting beat by a 17 year old?" I'd say. "When I'm your age, nobody in the world will be able to beat me!" That would infuriate them, and they'd be pulling their pockets inside out looking for more money to try me again.

My third advantage was my stamina, which was tremendous. I could—and sometimes did—bowl all night without getting tired, and that gave me an edge over just about anyone I played. Some betting sets were just for three, five or six games, but a lot were like poker, where you hung in there and played as long as the guy, or guys, who were losing wanted to keep going. With my size (I was a full six-foot-two inches tall and 180 pounds when I was 16 years old) and my farm-boy strength, I could stay with anybody. Many was the night that I'd take on three or four different opponents over a total of 50 games or more, and walk away whistling while they lay sprawled on the benches.

Things were going so well for me around Chicago that the summer before my senior year at Crane Tech I took my show on the road, to Miami, Florida. A neighborhood buddy, Jimmy Chakos, and I got in my car and drove down there on a couple hundred dollars I persuaded my mom to give me. We checked into a hotel on Collins Avenue in Miami Beach (not the best, but a pretty good one) and soaked up the sun for a couple of days. Then we sallied forth looking for bowling action.

Neither Jimmy nor I had ever been to Miami, but that

didn't bother us. We let our fingers do the walking, opening the telephone Yellow Pages and picking out the bowling center with the biggest ad. It was a place called Lounge Bowl. We walked in at about noon and marched up to the counter. "I'm Carmen Salvino from Chicago, and I'd like to take on your best bowlers," I told the man at the cash register. "I'll bowl 'em for $50 or $100. I'll bowl 'em for $5 if that's all they've got. Tell 'em I'll be back tonight after the leagues are over."

The guy just laughed. "Okay, I'll tell 'em," he said.

At 10 p.m. I was back, just like I'd promised. The fellow behind the counter was surprised. "I thought you were kidding," he said.

"I'll show you how I'm kidding," said I. Jimmy and I got ourselves a lane and started to bowl. Pretty soon people were gathering around. One fellow offered to bowl me three games for $50. I beat him. Another guy made me the same offer, and I beat him, too. Then a tall, skinny guy named Mike Prognowsky came up to me. "I'll bowl you for $100, but not here," he said. "We gotta go to another center."

Now I don't recommend that anyone do what I did, which was say "yes" to an offer like that. Later in life I learned to be very wary about bowling someone I didn't know on his own turf. In fact, I should have learned that lesson myself with my experience with Lefty Masera at G & L Lanes in Chicago. But I was young and brave and had money in my pocket. So I agreed.

We got into his car and drove across town to his home center. He was a left-hander and had a favorite pair of lanes on which no one could beat him. In the warmups I found out why: It was just about impossible to control a ball from anywhere but the left–center of the lanes, where he liked to bowl. But a bet was a bet, and I had to make the best of it. Instead of bowling from my usual spots, I set up on the left and angled my hook toward the right gutter, from where it hooked into the pocket. I guess no right-hander ever did that to Prognowsky before, because it seemed to amaze and confuse him. I didn't bowl all that great, but he bowled worse, and I won.

We went back to the Lounge Bowl every night for a week after that, and found a steady stream of people who wanted to try me. I beat just about all of them. Then, inevitably, the competition began to thin out. About the middle of the second week, I found myself without a match and ready to go home. An older fellow at the lanes named Hoagie, who'd been watching me a lot of nights, said he thought that would be a shame. He proposed to set up a match with me as his partner against a couple of the better bowlers around town that he'd been wanting to beat for years.

I didn't like the sound of that, and I told him so. He said he had about a 175 average, and from the couple of times I'd watched him bowl, I believed it. I didn't want to have to average better than 225 to give us a chance to beat the pair of 200-average bowlers—Bill White and "Bones" Saunders—he wanted to match us against. He said not to worry, that he'd put up our side of the bet, which was to be $150 a man. He liked the action, and was willing to pay to be a part of it. On top of that, he offered to pay for my practice lines at the center where the match was to be held. Naturally, White and Saunders jumped at the chance for an easy payday.

I couldn't pass up a deal like that either, so I showed up at the center the morning of the match, and started practicing. By evening, I'd bowled about 50 lines at 50 cents each. Hoagie nearly collapsed when I presented him with a twenty-five-dollar bill for lines. ''We'll have to beat those guys for me to break even,'' he moaned.

The match started and Hoagie began knocking down pins like the best Classic League pro. We bowled three, three-game sets and won 'em all at $50 per. Hoagie's 209 average beat everybody, including me. You never saw such a happy fellow. He was so glad to beat those two guys, and to bowl as well as he did—his best showing ever, he said—that he gave me all our winnings, $300. That made it a $325 day for me, including the $25 in lines that Hoagie had paid for. Just as valuable was the lesson the evening taught, which was never to underestimate an opponent. Fortunately for me, I learned it at White and Saunders' expense.

Back in Chicago for my senior year of high school and, that spring, my initiation into the Classic League, I discovered the local version of Hustler's Heaven: Marigold Bowl. It was on Grace Street and Broadway Avenue on the city's North Side, across the street from Marigold Arena, where wrestling and boxing matches were staged. From about eleven o'clock in the evening, when the leagues ended, until three or four o'clock in the morning, and on weekends, any bowler, with any average, could get a game there for just about any amount of money he cared to wager.

Fred Fagenholz owned Marigold Bowl. He always dressed in black, which gave him a gangster appearance. Also, the place was headquarters for a platoon of gamblers and bookies, who took and placed bets on every sport you could name in addition to participating in the bowling action. But Fred was a 100-percent-square guy who made sure that no funny business took place *on* his lanes. If you walked into Marigold and said you were a 150-average bowler looking for a game, you'd get it. But if anyone discovered you were really a 180 bowler looking to score a few easy dollars, your health insurance would be put to the ultimate test.

Not only was there action aplenty above ground at Marigold, but also below ground next door. The coffee shop next to the place was owned by one Mike Cravello. It had a trap door in the floor of a utility room that led downstairs to a basement we called "Cravello's Dungeon." You could get into any kind of card game you wanted down there, free from the threat of interference by police. At 3 or 4 a.m., when the bowling would break up, we'd head down there, usually for poker or gin rummy, which became my specialty. The stakes usually were higher than they had been upstairs on the lanes.

Some of the guys who hung out in the Dungeon were rough characters, to say the least. One who stands out in my mind was nicknamed "Tomatoes." He was a band drummer by profession, although I never could figure out when he had time to play, because as far as I could see, he was downstairs playing cards at every hour of the day or night. Tomatoes always carried a gun, which he used to shoot the rats that sometimes ran along the walls in the place. He had a violent temper, and would bite his hands when he was losing. Sometimes he'd bite them so hard they'd bleed. He'd bet on anything: Once I heard him offer to put $1,000 on which of two flies on a wall would take off first. He offered to play gin rummy with me a couple of times, but I always turned him down, politely. I thought that beating him might be worse than losing.

All through my last year in high school, and during my first few years in the Classic League, I'd show up at Marigold at least three or four nights a week. In fact, after the Classic

League and North End Traveling League finished up on the week nights, a lot of the bowlers would troop over to Marigold, looking for action. Usually, we'd bowl against one another, individually or in various team combinations. The stakes never were very high, and I can't think of anyone who was a large and consistent winner in those games. But it was always a kick going against Bill Bunetta, Stan Gifford or Robby Robinson with $20 on the line and a lot of people watching. It was high noon in Dodge City...my kind of scene.

Other excellent bowlers who weren't well known for one reason or another would hang out at Marigold. For them, the late-night action was the Classic League and ABCs all rolled into one. I had some of my most memorable matches against those men. One of them was Oscar Stevenson, a most unusual guy.

Oscar was maybe a 185-average bowler in league play, which wasn't good enough to land him a spot in any of the major leagues. But team bowling was not his forte, match play was. He was a thin guy, and about 40 years old when I bowled him. He wasn't muscular, but very wiry, and had tremendous stamina. Once he bowled in a marathon and stayed on the lanes for six hours after everybody else in the contest had quit. When he finished game number 248, he turned around and asked the proprietor if he'd broken the house record. "Yeah, about 100 games ago," the proprietor said.

Oscar would beat higher-average bowlers by wearing them down. He'd lose about two of every three games for the first couple of hours, but he'd grow stronger while the guy he'd be bowling against would get weaker. One thing that sustained him was a hatred of losing that was almost pathological. The wall next to Lane 32 at Marigold—the end lane where a lot of the big-money matches were played—had dents in it from where Oscar would beat his fists after losses. There was no danger playing him, though, because he never got really mad at anyone but himself.

With my reputation around Marigold, Oscar and I soon bumped into each other. I was 18 years old at the time, and already a Classic League ace. We started our match at about 11:30 p.m. for $5 a game. We bowled 25 games and I won 20 of them, including the last 13 in a row.

"Oscar," I said, "the only way you're going to beat me is to roll a 300." The next game, that was exactly what he did! Nobody cheered for him louder than I, because Marigold gave a $50 prize to anyone who bowled 300 in the place before witnesses, and I thought I'd have that $50 in my pocket before the night, or day, was done.

We continued bowling, and I continued winning most of the games. In one of them I needed three strikes in the tenth frame to beat him by one pin. I popped three beauties, and Oscar went crazy. He stuck his head through the hoop that slowed down the balls coming into the rack, like he wanted to hang himself. A ball was rolling towards him, and I grabbed hold of his legs and started to pull. He hung on to the hoop with all his might. The ball would have brained him if a spectator hadn't run out and blocked it. It would have been a first in the annals of suicide.

Eventually he calmed down and let me pull his head out. It was getting close to daylight, and I was $100 or so ahead. I went to pack my bowling balls and go home. "Where are you going? This game ain't over yet!" he screamed. I shrugged my shoulders, unzipped my bag, and went back to the lanes.

We bowled until 5 p.m.—17½ hours in all. Then people began coming to bowl their leagues, and we had to leave. I was ahead by close to $150. I told him I was going home, and this time I meant it. That didn't suit Oscar. He started lighting matches and setting fire to the score sheets we had lying around! We couldn't pay our line fees without the sheets, and I couldn't figure out exactly how much money I'd won, so I threw the sheets on the floor and stamped out the fires while trying to hold off Oscar. The guy behind the counter didn't know whether to call the police or the fire department. You can believe me when I tell you I haven't had many matches like that one.

One of the biggest money matches I ever played took place at Marigold Bowl later that same year. My opponent was Ira Deacon, another fellow who wasn't a brilliant league bowler because he preferred the action of man-to-man play. I have to say that beating him gave me more satisfaction than beating Oscar Stevenson, partly for the money involved—I won about $500 altogether (remember, this was the early 1950s, when $500 was worth about what $2,500 is today)—and partly because I liked pulling his chain.

Even by the standards of a sport in which a certain amount of heckling and needling are accepted, Deacon was an artist at it. His habit was to grab the microphone they kept at the front desk at Marigold for announcements, and insult the guy he wanted a match with. One night he got on the thing and challenged me to a match on Lanes 31 and 32 for $100. He called me a showoff and a loud mouth, which were true, and a dummy, which wasn't. But it wasn't so much what he said as the way that he said it.

I said, "Okay, come on, I'll bowl you." He'd got me sore, and that was a mistake. I went out and bowled 774 for a three-game series, beating him by more than 100 pins. He didn't know how to handle that. He said, "You're a one-way bowler. All you know how to do is throw hard. You'll never make it big as a pro because you won't be able to handle all the different lane conditions."

"Oh, yeah?" I said. I picked up my ball, gripped it along the side without putting my fingers in the holes, and eased it down the lane. All the pins fell.

Well, that got him even madder still, and he challenged me to a rematch the next night. Naturally, I accepted. By the time the match came up, every gambler and bookmaker in the place seemed to have money riding on the outcome. I know that one fellow bet $2,000 on me and another bet $1,000. I had $100 of the betting action myself besides the $100 we were playing for. I wouldn't be surprised if $5,000 or $6,000 had been bet altogether.

This time the match was close. He shot a 685 and I had a 701. It came down to the last frames of the last game. I strung four strikes in a row to make sure that he couldn't catch me. I won $100 from Deacon and $100 on my bet, plus $300 that a couple of the bigger gamblers gave me for making their wagers good. It was quite a lucrative night's work for that time and place.

I know that by now you're thinking, "What's with this Salvino? Didn't he ever lose?" Sure I lost, plenty of times. Everybody has "down" nights, and I had my share. Also, surviving as a traveling professional bowler meant that you had to know when and where to open your mouth, and how to walk out of a place with your money in your pocket and the locals smiling and waving goodbye. More than once I took smaller bites out of people than I might have because my instincts told me that caution was the better part of valor.

I credit never getting into any serious scrapes over gambling to my Chicago-Florida boyhood. The Chicago part taught me how to handle myself in the big cities, and the Florida part how to handle the small-town types. I guess it stemmed, too, from my not being a greedy sort. Winning always was the most important thing for me. Money was just the way to keep score.

A lot of my betting games, in fact, were against other pros—guys on my own level in every way. My favorite foe was Johnny King, a fellow Classic Leaguer. He was a first-rate bowler in both the leagues and man-to-man matches, and if I came out ahead of him lifetime, it couldn't have been by much. Moreover, whatever I won from him on the lanes he almost always took back from me playing gin rummy. He was one of the best card players ever among the bowling pros, which is saying quite a lot.

The kicker in playing cards or bowling against "Kingy," as everybody called him, was that he would rather cheat you than beat you fairly. He had the heart and guts of a burglar. You couldn't get mad at him, though, because of the kind of person he was. He'd insult you in a way that would make you laugh, and he was such a soft touch that he'd give money to just about anyone with a story. He was a nice-looking guy who had an English accent even though he came from Cleveland. Women flocked around him like kids around a Good Humor truck. The guys who hung around with him were very glad to accept his leftovers.

You always had to watch yourself playing any game with Kingy. At cards, he could deal from any part of the deck with equal dexterity, and when you bowled against him he'd slip rosin or grease into the finger holes of your ball on critical frames. He was a master gamesman as well. Once he had a television match with Glenn Allison, a top-flight, veteran pro. Allison was a spot bowler who liked to pick a mark at the foul line for his release instead of one farther down the lane, the way most spot bowlers do. The match went down to the tenth frame with Allison needing a strike to win. As Allison was taking his approach, Kingy moved in front of a battery of TV lights, casting a shadow across the foul line and blocking Allison's spot. Allison's ball missed the pocket, and Kingy got the winner's check.

Kingy was involved, glancingly, in the one time that gamblers asked me to throw a match. He and I were booked to play a three-game set in a Rochester, New York, bowling center for a $500 first prize in 1954 or '55. When I arrived to warm up, I was approached by a couple of nicely dressed guys I'd never seen before. They told me they'd bet a few thousand dollars on King, and there would be $1,000 in it for me if I would make sure they won. They pointed out that I'd take home twice as much money by losing as by winning.

I told them to bug off. I'd never been involved in anything like that before, and I wasn't about to start. I'd known gamblers, of course; a lot of them hung around Marigold, and I knew there was betting on a lot of the Classic League matches. As I've said, sometimes I'd bet on myself to win in man-to-man matches, and on a few occasions gamblers would give me, and other bowlers, a cut of their winnings when they'd cashed an especially large wager on one of us.

But I never entertained the notion of intentionally losing to someone to win a bet. After I chased away those gamblers in Rochester, I asked Kingy if he knew anything about their deal. If he'd have said yes, I would have punched him out and called the cops on him. But he said it was news to him, and I believed him. We went out and bowled, and I beat him narrowly with a score of 680 or thereabouts. I never again saw or heard from the guys who approached me.

This, however, is not to say that there weren't any shennanigans on the circuits. One fellow I met in my travels around the East in the early 1960s was named Iggy. He was a stereotypical New Yorker: funny, wise-mouthed, and always looking for an easy way to make a dollar. He was a really good bowler who might have become a top tournament pro if he had taken the game seriously. But he lacked the discipline to practice regularly or, even, show up on time for matches. His favorite bet-winning gimmick was to offer to beat guys bowling with either hand. He could do it, too; he's the only guy I ever knew who was every bit as good left-handed as he was righty.

Iggy used to tell a story about a time he agreed with some gamblers—real tough guys—to dump a match. He said he thought he'd make it look good by bowling pretty well at first and missing a few shots later to let the other fellow barely win, so going into the last three frames he was nine pins ahead. Iggy dumped a spare in the eighth, but so did the guy he was bowling. The same thing happened in the ninth. Suddenly it dawned on Iggy that the other guy was trying to lose, too! The gamblers he made the deal with were watching from in back of the benches, looking very unhappy. Visions of broken legs—his own—flashed in Iggy's mind.

As he stood up for the tenth frame, the only possible way out occurred to him. He picked up his ball, readied it for his approach, and dropped it on his big toe, breaking it and losing the match by default. It hurt like crazy, he said, but it was a bargain compared with what the gamblers would have done to him if he'd won.

The gambling scene among the bowling professionals started to fade out in the middle 1950s, when televised matches started to pump some real money into the sport and made familiar faces of some of us. It all but disappeared for most intents and purposes with the early 1960s, when the PBA tour became a paying proposition.

I pretty much gave up hustling in 1956, when I signed a contract to endorse bowling products and conduct instructional clinics for American Machine & Foundry Company. That was the first of several such arrangements I would have with manufacturers over the years. AMF didn't want me going around the country playing match games for money with their emblem on my back, and the Miami bowling proprietors, remembering my foray there as a 17 year old, specifically asked that I refrain from betting.

I went along without an argument. Enough tournament action was starting to brew to pay my bills and then some, and I, like others, recognized that hustling didn't fit the image of a first-class sport we were trying to project. I haven't bowled anyone for more than a Coca-Cola since I put my name on the dotted line for AMF. Of course, I've won a heckuva lot of Cokes in those years.

4

On the Road

The middle 1950s were a time of great change for bowling. Television was beginning to get seriously into live coverage of sporting events, and bowling, with its compact, static setting and easy-to-understand format, was a natural early focus for the medium. Also, momentum was building within professional bowling ranks for a tournament circuit that would give us the opportunity to cash in on the growing public enthusiasm for our sport that TV was helping to generate. It wouldn't be long before I would be playing big roles in both of those developments.

At the same time, I was in the process of changing my own life. In 1953, I met and began dating Virginia Morelli, whom I was to marry in 1955. I can't say that marriage immediately made a mature fellow of me; in fact, I don't think I can claim to be mature even at this writing, in my 54th year. But I know that marriage settled me down some, and hastened the end of my career as a hustler, if for no other reason than that it meant I could no longer stay out bowling to 4 a.m. most nights.

I met Ginny through Leon Woodman, a Classic League buddy. Leon and I were bowling one night at Faetz & Niesen Lanes on the North Side of Chicago, and he asked me to take a ride with him to a bowling center about 10 minutes away. He said he was going to see his wife there, and that she had a friend he wanted me to meet. He said this girl was terrific looking and an excellent bowler. That was a combination I couldn't pass up.

We got to the place and Leon pointed out this slim girl with a blonde streak in her hair. I liked her looks right away, and after I'd watched her bowl a few frames I was impressed with that, too. But you know how it is with young guys; you couldn't come right out and tell a girl you liked her. So when we were introduced, I had to make a wisecrack. "What's your bowling average?" I asked.

"About 185," she answered.

"Here's a nickel," I said. "Call me when you get good." She smiled at that.

(Ginny: "Smiled? I winced. I thought he was a real smart-aleck.")

The next week Leon brought me back to the center, and this time Ginny and I talked longer. I could tell I was making some headway with her. When I asked her if I could drive her home, her eyes lit up and she said yes.

(Ginny: "My eyes lit up? Well, maybe. It was a cold night, and it meant that I wouldn't have to take the bus home.")

When I got to her house, I told her I'd like to call her

for a date sometime. I asked for her telephone number. I didn't have a pencil or paper, so I blew on my car window and wrote her number in the steam with my finger.

(Ginny: "It was just like Carmen not to be prepared.")

I called Ginny the next night and invited her to bowl with me in a mixed-doubles event in the suburb of Berwyn. Some of my Classic League friends and their wives or girl-friends also were going to be in it. We went there together, and bowled three games. She beat me all three! In front of my pals! I figured it was a fluke, and took her over to Marigold Bowl, where I was working as an instructor. We bowled another game there. I had a 236. She had a 257!

I couldn't let this go on, so right away I got her back into my car and drove to the one place where I knew I was unbeatable: good old Schueneman & Flynn's. We bowled five games there, and I whipped her in every one. Then and there I made myself a promise to never again bowl against her, and I've kept it to this day. I think that's a big reason we've been happily married as long as we have.

(Ginny: "That and the fact that my beating him those first few times set him down a peg or two, even if I was bowling over my head. He became an easier person to like after that.")

Single or married, a bowling professional spends a lot of time on the road. Today, I usually travel by plane and stay at first-class hotels. Then, we not only traveled in our cars but a lot of times we also slept in them. I think that I've visited—and bowled in—just about every small city or town in the Midwest. Canton, Youngstown, Parma Heights, and Hubbard, Ohio; DeKalb, Springfield, Streator, East St. Louis, Aurora and Elgin, Illinois; all over Michigan, Iowa and Wisconsin. I bowled three-gamers, five-gamers and six-gamers for purses that rarely topped $500. Usually, they were weekend sweepstakes events, with the prize money coming from bowlers' entry fees after the proprietor had taken out his share for lines.

You had to be good to win those little tournaments, and lucky, too. The luck came in partly because a lot of them included bowlers with handicaps, and it was pretty rare when some fellow with, say, a 180 average wouldn't pop a freak 230 score or two and win the thing. You also had to be careful not to give the locals too much notice that you were coming, because some of them hated to see big-city hot-shots drive in and win their tournaments, and they'd trick up their lanes on you to the point of impossibility if they got the chance. The best strategy was to show up the day of the event, put your entry fee down, and hope that not too many people recognized you.

Conditions in some of those small-town bowling centers could be weird even when they weren't hoked up for the benefit of out-of-towners. I'll never forget a trip to the Pocono Mountains, in Pennsylvania, that I took in the winter of 1954 or '55 with Tony Gardini, who was my captain on the Chez Paree nightclub team in the North End Traveling League. We left Chicago on a Friday afternoon, spent the night in a motel in Ohio, and arrived before noon on Saturday in the Pennsylvania town where the first tournament was to be held. It was a real little town, and the bowling center was supposed to be on its only major street, but we cruised its whole length a couple of times without finding it. We stopped and asked for directions, and finally wound up in front of a place that looked like a normal, large, wood-frame house.

I knew this wasn't going to be my day the moment I opened the front door and banged my head on some bleachers that were just inside it. In what looked like somebody's rebuilt living room, dining room, kitchen and back porch were eight lanes. We paid our fees and were directed to a couple of them to warm up. On the first lane I tried, my ball hooked so much I couldn't believe it. All I could knock down were a couple of pins in the lefthand corner. The next lane didn't hook at all. You can't score in a place like that unless you grew up in it, and neither Tony nor I could do a thing when our turns came to bowl.

We shrugged, picked up our bags and headed for a near-by town and the second tournament on our list that day. We found the bowling center easily enough, paid our fees and asked for a warmup lane. ''Take number 13,'' said the man behind the desk.

We looked and saw that the lane numbers stopped at 12, and told the guy so. ''You didn't look hard enough,'' he said, pointing with his finger. Lane 13 was between lanes 10 and 11. The counter man, who also was the owner, explained that he was superstitious, and thought it was unlucky for his last lane to have the number 13.

We went out on the approach, and the light shining off the lanes was almost blinding. They'd not only put a ton of oil on them, but also Simonize! They were so gooey that there was sawdust in the pits where the ball returns were so that the pinsetters could dry the balls enough to return them to the bowlers! Not only were our shots sliding all over the place, but they also were bouncing off the pins, which weighed about five pounds each. I think I averaged 165 for my six games, and Tony about 160. Neither of us could believe it. I mean, we'd paid for gas and a motel room, bought a couple of meals and put up two sets of entry fees, and all we had to show for it were a couple of sticky bowling balls and a knot on my forehead from where I'd bumped it on the bleachers in that first place.

I was upset, but Tony was steaming. We got in my car at about seven o'clock in the evening. "I'm driving," Tony announced.

"Okay, you're the captain," I said. "Where do you want to stay tonight?"

"Nowhere. We're going back to Chicago," said Tony. "I'm not staying in this goddamned state another minute!"

He drove all the way home to Chicago—more than 900 miles—without stopping for anything but gas. We got to Tony's house just before nine o'clock on Sunday morning. He jumped out of the car without taking his suitcase or even turning off the motor. He ran upstairs and woke his wife from a sound sleep. The first words out of his mouth to her were "Didja ever bowl on ice?!" We never went back to the Poconos.

Another place I've never gone back to is Parma Heights, Ohio, but for a different reason. The last time I visited there, in 1954, I was made an official guest of the city in a way I didn't appreciate.

I was with the Tri Par Radio team, and we'd bowled an exhibition against a local crew. My roommate, Chuck Wagner, and I were in my car, driving back to our motel, when we passed a policeman giving a traffic ticket to a woman. I was in a kind of goofy mood, so I leaned out the window and yelled "Hey, give her a break!" at the cop. He turned to see who was shouting at him, and Wagner applied the finishing (for us) touch. "You dirty cop," Wagner said, loud enough for the cop to hear.

We parked our car in the motel lot and turned to see the cop coming for us. Chuck started to run for our room.

I did, too, more out of reflex than from any conviction it was a good idea. The cop, of course, didn't have to outrun us. "Stop or I'll shoot!" he hollered. We stopped.

He braced us against our car and started frisking us. "Where are you guys from?" he asked. We said Chicago. That was all he needed to hear. "A couple of Chicago hoods, huh?" said he. "Well, that stuff doesn't go down here."

While he was putting us into his squad car for the ride "downtown," Joe DiMichele, the sixth man on our team and an older fellow, came by. When he saw what was happening, he tried to smooth things over. "Look, these are young fellows, here for a bowling match," he told the cop. "They were just kidding around. Can I do something for you to make up for this?"

"I don't take bribes," the cop barked at Joe. "You come with me, too."

He drove all three of us to a fire station that had one cell. That was the local jail. This fat old guy, who said he was the justice of the peace, told us we were charged with disorderly conduct, and set our bail at $25 apiece. We phoned Art Butler, our captain, to come down and get us out. Art showed up right away with Joe Wilman and Joe Norris and put up the bail money, but not without first having a good laugh at our expense. Wagner and I were tickled to get out of there, but not the supposedly mature DeMichele. "This is a miscarriage of justice! I want my day in court!" he hollered. It took all five of us to shut him up and hustle him away before he got us into more trouble than we were in in the first place.

Starting the next year, 1955, I became well known enough that something like the Parma Heights incident probably couldn't have happened. I got to be a television star.

The program that did it was "Championship Bowling," which was started in 1952 on local Chicago television and soon was seen all over the United States. It was the biggest of several TV shows that were to make bowling television's number one sport in terms of hours on the tube by the late 1950s.

"Championship Bowling" was produced by Walter Schwimmer, a Chicago advertising man and television pioneer, and came out of Faetz & Niesen Bowling Center on the city's North Side. It first aired in the eleven-to-midnight slot on WMAQ-TV in Chicago, and did so well in the ratings that Schwimmer offered a 26-show package to the Big Three networks. They turned it down because they thought that bowling was strictly a participation sport that no one would want to watch.

Schwimmer then turned to syndication, but the early results weren't promising. In the first six months of 1963, he sold "Championship Bowling" to just four stations outside of Chicago. But one of them was in South Bend, Indiana, which put it on opposite the Pabst Blue Ribbon Wednesday night boxing matches, then the nation's top-rated sports show. Within a few weeks, "Championship Bowling" was outdrawing the fights in South Bend. Armed with that example, Schwimmer sold the show to about 100 stations in the next six months, a figure unheard of at the time. It was to remain on the air in one form or another until 1965.

A good part of "Championship Bowling's" success was due to Schwimmer's promotional talents. He put up a $10,000 prize for anyone who rolled a 300 game on the show. That was an enormous sum of money in those days, and stirred real interest. Steve Nagy got coast-to-coast headlines for the program—and professional bowling—when he shot a perfect game on a 1954 show to collect the big check. Another asset was the show's announcer, Joe Wilson, who got the nickname "Whispering Joe" from the way he whispered into the microphone so the bowlers wouldn't hear him during the matches. Wilson was almost as important to "Championship Bowling" as the bowlers. Instead of just showing up at broadcast time and following a script, he'd get there early to chat with us and learn about our backgrounds, personalities, and styles. That gave his commentaries special authority.

The bowlers who were the biggest attractions on "Championship Bowling" were the demonstrative ones, like Buzz Fazio, Therman Gibson, Steve Nagy, and me. Fazio was a real excitable guy under normal circumstances, and television brought out the showman in him fully. He'd get down on his knees and pray for a strike as his ball went down the lane, and lead the cheers for himself when the pins fell. Being short and having a great smile didn't hurt him, either. In the fall of 1955, he won seven straight live matches on "Championship Bowling, and the last few were reported in the newspapers as major athletic events. I recall reading somewhere that about two-thirds of the TV sets in Chicago were tuned to the Saturday-night programs during Buzz's streak, the highest rating any program had gathered to that time.

Gibson was an altogether different-looking sort from Fazio. He was stocky and bald-headed, not cute in any sense. But he had a habit of clapping his hands when he knew he was going to get a strike, and pretty soon bowlers all over the country were copying him in that.

Gibson won the biggest jackpot of televised bowling's younger days on a program that was called, aptly enough, "Jackpot Bowling." On Jan. 2, 1961, he took home $75,000 for rolling six straight strikes under a format in which the prize mounted every time the bowlers on the show failed to achieve that.

The funny twist about Gibson's "Jackpot Bowling" performance was that the program usually was taped, and he had promised to call his wife in advance and tell her if he'd won. But this time, for some reason, the show went on live. Therman's wife hadn't heard from him, so she sat at home watching, figuring that he was going to miss somewhere along the line. She almost had a heart attack when he got the sixth and final strike.

I was on "Championship Bowling" maybe 20 times over the years, and usually did well. My jumps and spins after I threw my ball made a big hit with a lot of people, although some thought they were somehow phony and called me a "hot dog" for doing them. I can assure you, like I assured people then, that all my antics on the lanes are completely spontaneous. I'd sit at home watching the taped shows and laugh at myself along with everyone else. It's funny about things like that, you know. When a young athlete is flamboyant, he's called a "hot dog" or, now, a "flake." When he's middle-aged and does the same things, he's "colorful." And when he's old and does them, he's "cute." I'm considered colorful now, but I'm afraid it won't be long before I'm cute.

My biggest television-show paycheck came on a program out of Chicago called "Bowling with the Stars." I was on for seven weeks in a row in 1954, and won $10,000 in prizes and bonuses. One week I shot a three-game score of 846, which as far as I know is the highest ever on a show of that kind. "Bowling with the Stars" was taped, with three programs being filmed in one day for showing later on a once-a-week basis. I remember getting a letter from a woman after one of those three-week stretches asking why I never changed my shirt.

As anyone who has been on television regularly can tell you, the medium can make you an instant celebrity. After my first few appearances in the early '50s, people began stopping me on the street or in restaurants for autographs. I liked it then, and like it now. I make it a point to be nice to people who approach me, because I want them to have a good impression of me and my sport. Some people are unreasonable, though. For example, when I'm at a urinal, I'm not about to drop everything so I can sign a piece of paper for someone. Believe me, I've been asked for autographs there plenty of times.

Those made-for-TV bowling shows are pretty much gone now, replaced by telecasts of the finals of PBA tournaments. The Saturday afternoon series in the winter, and some spring telecasts, had been on the ABC network for 26 consecutive years in 1987, making it TV's longest-running sports show, and NBC and ESPN carried PBA tourney telecasts as well. Bowling has long outrated a long list of other sports on the tube, including golf, tennis, hockey, soccer and boxing. This always comes as a surprise to some people, but it shouldn't. There are more than seven million registered bowlers in the United States, more than are signed up for any other sport. Moreover, I think that the PBA format, with five bowlers competing in a single-elimination ladder (the fifth-place bowler faces the fourth-placer, the winner faces the third-placer, and so on, with the survivor taking on the leader for the championship), is an excellent one, and the matches themselves are fast-paced and riveting. Unlike some other sports, including football, bowling hasn't had to make a lot of changes in recent years to make itself more palatable for television. I think that's a tribute to the game we have fashioned.

It's also a tribute to Eddie Elias, the Akron, Ohio, lawyer who organized the PBA and did more than any other man to make it work. I can speak authoritatively on this subject, because I was in on the formation of the PBA and just completed a term, covering 1985 and 1986, as its president. Also, Eddie is my agent and dear friend. He's the Pete Rozelle and Peter Ueberroth of professional bowling rolled into one.

To understand what the PBA means to professional bowlers, a word about what things were like before it existed is in order. Before the organization was formed in 1958, we players had very little voice in where or when we bowled, or under what conditions. The major annual tournaments were run by the ABC and BPAA. The ABC is the national organization for men's bowling in the United States. It makes the rules, authenticates records, and organizes national competitions for its entire membership, which reached a peak of 4.8 million in 1980-81. That didn't give it an awful lot of time to spend on the wishes and problems of a couple hundred professionals. The BPAA is made up of people who own and operate bowling centers, and it has other concerns as well. It wasn't that those two organizations didn't want to help us pros, it was that their other responsibilities came first.

The classic or major leagues in the big cities of the Midwest and East were the major source of week-in, week-out competition for most of us, but the prize money they offered was governed by attendance, and since few bowling centers had any seating capacity to speak of, it usually was small. The companies that sponsored the teams would offer a set amount of annual expense money, which team members could use pretty much as they wished for travel and tournament-entry fees.

As a bowler got better, he could move to a better-financed team. For instance, Alcazar Hotel, my first Classic League outfit, received $1,500 a year all told, and my Meister Brau team got $10,000. Munsingwear, which sponsored a crack unit in the late 1950s (besides me, the members were Buddy Bomar, Morrie Oppenheim, Bill Bunetta and Jack Biondolillo) put up $15,000 a year, plus, naturally, shirts and slacks. But not shoes or balls; we had to get those on our own. And, like I said before, we had to split the prize money we won from any source with our teammates. I don't think my team take ever topped $8,000 a year.

In addition, until the PBA came along, there was no agreement on what a professional bowler was. At one time, the ABC defined a pro as a person who earned 50 percent of his income from bowling, but that included a lot of fellows who stood behind the counter in bowling stores, and some of them couldn't play worth a darn. Now, the PBA says that a pro is someone who has had a certified 190 average for two years in ABC-sanctioned league play, and is of good character. Anyone who meets those standards, and has cashed in two PBA regional tournaments, can enter the qualifying rounds of a national tour event.

The first time I met Eddie Elias was at a meeting in the winter of 1958 during the BPAA national doubles championships in Mountainside, New Jersey. Eight of us pros were there: me, Don Carter, Dick Weber, Buzz Fazio, Steve Nagy, Pat Patterson, Billy Welu and Dick Hoover, who was from Akron, the same as Eddie. Dick introduced him, and Eddie began to talk. For one reason or another some of the guys weren't paying attention. That got me angry, and I grabbed an empty soda pop bottle that was laying around and banged it on a table. "Let this guy talk," I said. "He paid his own way here, and we owe him at least that courtesy. What he has to say might benefit all of us one day."

Eddie told us that if we ever wanted to get anywhere, we'd have to have our own organization, one that was working exclusively for us, and that we'd have to get our tournaments on television. He said we needed TV because bowling wasn't—and probably would never be—like baseball or football, which are played in stadiums before large, paying audiences and could get along on gate receipts. He also told us that we'd have to tie up with corporate sponsors if we wanted to get our purse money up to near where it was in golf or tennis. He was way ahead of his time on that point.

He said that while his hometown of Akron wasn't a major city, he had some contacts that would help him get our feet in both the TV and corporate-sponsorship doors. He named the comedian Danny Thomas, who was of Lebanese extraction like Eddie, and Firestone Tire & Rubber Company, with which he'd done considerable business. Finally, he was clear about what would be in it for him: He wanted to run our organization and get a share of whatever television money he brought in. He scored some points for candor there.

We told him we'd think it over and get back to him, but my mind was pretty much made up. I'd already been thinking along the same lines Eddie had laid out. Also, I was impressed with him as a person. His eyes, voice, and mannerisms all made me believe that he could deliver what he'd outlined. I and some of the other fellows checked out the things he'd told us about himself, and we got confirmations right down the line.

Eddie spoke to a larger group of us in May of that year

in Syracuse, New York. He said that he would set up a short tourney circuit the next year, and that he was working on a group insurance plan for us, the first ever for pro bowlers. About 75 guys were at that meeting, and most of them weren't exactly bowled over. Only 33 of us—me included—antied up the $50 that it took to be a PBA charter member. But the organization was launched.

The PBA's first "circuit," in 1959, consisted of three tournaments that offered a total of $49,500 in prize money. The first, the Empire State in Albany, New York, had a first prize of $2,500. In a way, it got us off on the wrong foot, because it was won by "Wrong Foot" Lou Campi, so nick-named because he was a right-hander who delivered his ball off his right foot. I still don't know how he did it. The other two tourneys that year, the Paramus-Eastern in Paramus, New Jersey, and the Dayton Open in Dayton, Ohio, were won by Dick Weber.

The next year, 1960, the tour had seven stops worth $150,000. Those figures climbed to 11 tourneys worth $250,000 in 1961. In 1962, we had 32 tournaments worth $800,000, and our winter finals went on ABC-TV for the first time. Total purse money topped the $1 million mark in 1963. By 1986, the PBA oversaw 130 national and regional events and distributed $6.5 million in prizes. Twenty-eight bowlers won $50,000 or more in 1986, which was more than Dick Weber won as the PBA's leading money winner 21 years before. I think it's safe to say that the PBA tour is here to stay.

Unfortunately, that wasn't the fate of the other great experiment of that period, the National Bowling League (NBL). The NBL was formed in 1961 by a group of men who thought that the sport could be taken out of the regular bowling centers and put into arenas where people would pay to watch it. According to the *National Bowlers Journal,* they put up $14 million to learn if their guess was correct. It wasn't, but not because I didn't do my best to make it work.

I know how youngsters coming out of college to play professional football or basketball feel, because the teams that made up the NBL got started with a player draft, and I was picked by the Fort Worth team. I didn't especially like the idea of being told by someone else where I had to play, and I let the Fort Worth people know this. They traded my "rights" to a group out of Birmingham, Alabama. I dickered with them for awhile, but they lost their financial backing before a deal could be struck. Then the Dallas team picked me up.

Dallas was a far more attractive proposition than the other two teams. Lamar Hunt owned the team, named the Broncos, and he did things first-class. He flew me to Dallas to meet with Curtis Sanford, his general manager. Sanford offered me $20,000 for a 12-week season, and got me and my family a place to live in a beautiful apartment complex owned by the Hunt family. He even bought me a 10-gallon hat.

Sanford took me to see Bronco Bowl, where the team would play. The place was terrific: Six lanes bounded on three sides by 3,000 theater-type seats that gave everyone a perfect view of the action. It was the sort of setup I'd dreamed about, both for myself and the sport. That clinched it. I put my name on the dotted line.

The NBL format was different from anything that had been tried in bowling. Instead of five guys on a team, like in other leagues, we were permitted as many as 10, with free substitutions. A team captain could call in a sub to pick up a single spare, such as a left-hander for a 10-pin, or replace a bowler who was doing poorly. Each man, or his sub, would roll two games instead of the usual three, and in direct competition with one guy from the other team. Instead of just counting total scores, like in normal league play, teams would get points for match-play results, margins of victory, and bonuses for things like rolling three or more strikes in a row. Scores would come out as 33-25, or 24-17. The idea was to get the spectators rooting for the results of each individual match or, even, each ball.

The NBL's most-novel aspect was that the fans were encouraged to cheer and boo at any time, much like in baseball, football, and basketball. That was a real wrench for me and the other bowlers. As much as I wanted to make the fans feel that they were a part of things, I could never get used to them hollering while I was going to the line.

In some cities, they did more than holler. Dallas's big rival was the Fort Worth team I had turned down initially, and when the Broncos went there to bowl the first time, the yahoos were out in force. One group of people would stamp their feet in unison when a Dallas bowler went to the line, in time with his footwork. The next time they'd speed up their stamping to try to throw him off. There were lots of insults directed at us, and worse. Once I looked up into the crowd to see a guy with his hands cupped over his mouth, turned towards where Ginny, my wife, was sitting. It looked like he was hassling her. I climbed into the stands, grabbed the guy by the shoulders, and shook him pretty good. There was no real fight, because people pulled us apart before anyone could throw any punches. But I was fined $400 by the league, and the incident made all the papers. The next week, when we bowled in Los Angeles, someone from the crowd threw a paper box at me as I got up to bowl. I opened it to find a pair of boxing gloves. "Hey, Salvino! Why don't you try bowling with those on?" yelled the guy who threw them. I laughed along with everybody else.

I also tried to get publicity for the league in more conventional ways. In Omaha, the day before we were to bowl the home-town team captained by Buzz Fazio, my old buddy and sparring partner, I was interviewed by a local television station about the condition of the lanes. "They stink," I said. "Fazio has tricked them up to give his team an edge." I said it partly because it was true—Buzz had oiled the lanes to a high shine to suit his straight-ballers—and because I knew it would get the locals stirred up and increase attendance.

Mostly, I boosted the league by bowling well and being my normal, active self. The best publicity the NBL ever got was a spread of photographs in *Sports Illustrated* magazine. Most of the pictures were of me, jumpin' and jivin'. I led the league in average until the final week of the season, and finished first in a number of other statistical categories.

Alas, the NBL never finished its first campaign. It didn't get the television contract it needed to survive, and some of the leading bowlers, including Don Carter and Dick Weber, never could be persuaded to join. The schedule was cut off about a month before it was supposed to end. Several of the teams didn't make it that far.

Some of the players didn't get all the money they'd been promised by the NBL team owners, but I wasn't one of them. Lamar Hunt paid me my entire $20,000. I hadn't signed the league's biggest contract at the beginning of the season, but I think I wound up getting the most money. That was the first and last time I ever bowled competitively for a salary—a disappointment because I liked the feeling. Players in team sports have it good in that respect. The epilogue to the NBL story was almost as sad. Beautiful Bronco Arena in Dallas was turned into a roller-skating place, and then a dance hall. Bowling never had such a perfect showcase.

In the meantime, I was doing pretty well on the new PBA tour. My first tournament victory with the organization came in 1961, when I won the Empire State to open the season. First prize was $3,000. The next year I won the Pontiac Open in Michigan after walking through a glass door and cutting my head, hand and arm on the first day of the tournament.

Later in 1962 I captured what was to be my most prestigious tour crown, the PBA Nationals at Boulevard Lanes in Philadelphia. The circumstances surrounding that win, and the guy who gave me the tip that saved it, made it one of my more unusual victories.

I went into that tournament in anything but the best frame of mind. Ginny and I had a nasty argument several days before I was to leave for Philadelphia, and I'd moved out of our apartment into a hotel in downtown Chicago. I can't recall now what the fight was about, and if the history of our early-marriage squabbles held true, I probably didn't remember the subject two or three days after it occurred. I do know that the odds were about 10-to-1 that I was to blame.

That's usually the story when professional athletes fight with their wives, I've noticed. To reach the top of a big-time pro sport, you have to have a big ego and tunnel vision, and be able to administer the *coup de grace* to a wobbly opponent. None of those characteristics go over big around the house. Neither does the fact that the typical jock gets pats on the back aplenty from fans and hangers-on during his work day and expects his wife to continue the cheering when he comes home. Ginny deserves a medal for putting up with me until I got smart enough to realize that my life with her and Corinne was just as important as what I was up to on the lanes.

I was irritable and didn't practice well before the Nationals, but as the tournament unfolded I got better and better, and qualified ninth or tenth for one of the 24 places in the finals. I led the field through the first several rounds of match play, but suddenly my game went sour and I skidded to sixth place with six games to go. I had to move up to at least fourth to get into the championship round under the format in place at the time.

I was sitting in the locker room, trying to figure out what I was doing wrong, when Buzz Fazio approached. I'd just beaten him by a couple of pins with about a 195 score in a match in which neither of us had bowled well. He had no chance to win at that point but I still was in the chase, and Buzz was the sort of fellow who'd do anything he could to beat you, but anything he could to help you after a contest was over. He told me I was holding my ball too far out front and that this was putting me off balance on my approach.

I corrected the fault Buzz had spotted, and started getting strikes again. I headed into my final two-game set against Georgie Howard, a stylish veteran, back in first place, but with Don Carter right behind me in second and Howard a close third. Under the complicated pins-and-match results system then in use, I had to beat Howard solidly to win because Carter had a better match-game record than I did.

Howard did his best that last set, rolling games of 227 and 236. Carter did even better, winning his match with scores of 256 and 258. I rolled a 248 followed by a 279 that included five straight strikes to start and five more to finish. I beat Carter by 64 pins in the overall count, but with the won-lost records tossed in I edged him on the scoreboard by a bare .19-point.

The first thing I did after I left the lanes in Philadelphia was phone Ginny. I apologized to her for acting stupid. She said all was forgiven. She also told me to pin my winner's check of $6,500 to something big so I wouldn't lose it. "Lose that check and you're in *real* trouble," said she.

Something else that I did in 1962 turned out to be more important for me even than beating Carter and winning the Nationals. I went overseas for the first time in my life, to Japan. It was on a promotional trip arranged by Ebonite, for which I was working at the time. Carter also went, along with Ebonite executive Harry Davis. The idea was to help popularize bowling in Japan, where it was just catching on, and, naturally, to make sure that as many of the new Japanese bowlers as possible bought Ebonite gear.

I thought this would be just another bowling trip, only longer, but I was in for a lot of surprises. I knew that something special was up the moment we got off the plane in Tokyo. There must have been 500 little kids at the airport, waving American flags behind a big sign in Japanese and English that read, "Welcome, World's Greatest Bowlers." I knew that meant Carter, and I looked around to see if Dick Weber had stowed away on the plane. When I didn't see him, I figured the sign must be for me, too.

There was a press conference, with about 100 photographers shooting off flashbulbs at us. The reporters were very polite, addressing us as "Salvino, San" and "Carter, San." ("San" means "sir" in Japanese.) That was a big contrast with the American bowling writers, with whom we were on a "hey, you" basis.

We were driven to our hotel and told that a party was

to be staged in our honor that night. "Go to your loom, change clothes, and meet us in the robby," our Japanese host said. I thought, "What's a loom? What's a robby?" Then it dawned on me that was Japanese English. I was doing it myself before I left the country.

I rushed upstairs and changed clothes quickly, tired from the long plane ride and not looking too closely at what I was putting on. At the night club they seated us men in every other seat. Before I could dope out what that was all about, young hostesses began filling in the empty places. When I'd left Chicago, Ginny had told me to "have a good time, but not too good," so I was watching myself, trying not to get too friendly with the females. After a few minutes the woman sitting next to me would smile and leave, and another would take her place, while the women next to the guys who were smiling and chatting with them would stay put. I asked Davis, who had visited Japan before, about that, and he told me our hosts were trying to make sure we had a good time by matching us with compatible girls. You showed you liked your girl by smiling and talking. I got with the program better after that.

The evening went on and, in the normal course of things, Davis and Carter excused themselves to go to the washroom. They motioned for me to join them. I thought that was a bit strange, but I went. I thought it was stranger still that they were giggling and poking one another all the way there, but when we arrived I found out why. It was a co-ed toilet, men and women together, and no doors on the stalls.

I got in line for a urinal, and when my turn came I got another surprise: In my haste to dress at the hotel, I'd put my boxer shorts on backwards. I fumbled around for a few moments, shrugged my shoulders, and sheepishly told Harry and Don I couldn't go. "You Italian lovers are alike—all talk," Harry laughed.

About a half-hour later the call of nature became too strong to deny, so I had to go back to the washroom, take off my pants and shorts, and put them on again right. The men and women who watched me were chuckling behind their hands, and I was plenty embarrassed. For the rest of the evening, every time someone in the night club laughed, I was sure he or she was laughing at me.

The next day it was out on the lanes for Don and me, and it was our turn to teach the Japanese our customs. We bowled a straight match first, before a large and attentive, but very quiet, crowd. It quickly occurred to me that the people didn't know when they should cheer or applaud, so when Don was bowling I'd go and sit in the audience, and when he'd roll a strike or spare, I'd clap real loud. Pretty soon the people got the idea and started doing it on their own.

To spice up the program, I put on a show, demonstrating how I could make my ball hook in various ways. That got a big response, including laughter as well as applause. I included that routine in all our subsequent appearances. Before I left Japan, I made an hour-long bowling instructional tape that was translated into Japanese and, I was told, distributed by "Tom" Horiike, who headed a chain of bowling centers in Japan. That so impressed the Japanese that they insisted I be included in every later tour of their country by American bowlers. I eventually learned enough about Japanese customs to be the middleman between the bowlers and the Japanese on those trips. When one of our guys would do something the Japanese considered impolite, like talking too loudly or winking at the wrong girls, they'd come to me about it, and I'd talk to the bowler. Between 1962 and the end of 1987, I'd visited Japan 13 times.

I look forward to more trips to Japan, because I never fail to come home from there feeling better than when I left. They're a quieter people than we are, and, seemingly, more at ease with themselves. Maybe it's because there are 120 million of them packed onto an island the size of the state of Montana, but they treat one another with more respect and consideration than we in the United States do. In Japan, for instance, no one ever pours his own beer at a restaurant, because his dining companions do it for him. I like the custom of bowing to older people, too. The older you are in Japan, the lower bow you rate. They were bowing to their waists for me on my last trip. If I don't hurry back, their heads'll be scraping the floors the next time.

My only other foreign bowling trips were to Venezuela, where the PBA sent a couple of delegations in the late 1960s. That was a quite-different experience from my Japanese visits. The first time I was in that country was in 1967 to bowl a tournament. Our plane landed at the airport in Caracas, and we went through customs without any trouble. But on the way to our taxis a policeman outside pointed at the bowling-ball bag I was carrying and asked me to open it. I'd heard about the high humidity in Caracas, so I'd brought along a blank ball with the intention of drilling finger and thumb holes after I arrived in case my hands swelled.

The cop had me take the ball out of my bag. Without the holes, it looked like a cannonball you'd see in the Saturday morning television cartoon shows. He began hollering a word in Spanish that sounded like "Bomb!" and motioned to other cops to come look. A couple of them had machine guns and used them to shove me over to a wall. They made me turn and put my hands on the wall while they searched me.

Let me tell you, it was one confused scene. I was hollering "Bowling ball! Bowling ball!" and sweating pretty good, because it's no fun having machine guns pointed at you. Some of the other American bowlers came running over. About half of them were laughing while the other half were trying to help. Our translator finally arrived to fix things up, but not before a fair-sized crowd had gathered, not all of it friendly looking. Needless to say, I was glad to get out of there.

The Venezuelan bowling people were very apologetic and did all they could to make the rest of our trip enjoyable. They were so nice that I returned to the country for an official PBA tournament, the Venezuelan Invitational, the following year. About a dozen U.S. pros, including Weber, Johnny King, Harry Smith and Billy Welu, also made the trip, so it was a good field.

We got out of the airport smoothly this time, but the atmosphere at the tournament was unusual, to say the least. Bowlers from Latin America also were in the field, and they brought their fans with them. Some of them did their best to throw us "Yanquis" off our games.

I remember a pair of kids in the audience one day I was bowling. One of them had a little metal cricket that would go "click-click" when he pushed it. Every time I'd make my approach he'd click away in time with my steps. About the time I got used to that, the other kid pulled out a harmonica and played it!

Some of us Americans compounded our problems by taking too much of a liking to the local mixed drinks. Dick Weber, who wasn't a big drinker, had one or two rum concoctions with his dinner, and when we bowled together later that evening he was leaning so far to the right he looked like the Leaning Tower of Pisa. But he still bowled well enough to beat me in our head-to-head.

Not many other guys in Caracas got the best of me, though, and I won the tournament. My check came to $1,800. It was the smallest first-place prize on the tour that year, but it was welcome nonetheless. I hadn't been bowling well, and my money winnings dropped to just $12,337—including the Caracas check—from $28,170 the year before. I thought the win might be the charm I needed to turn things around. I couldn't have been more wrong.

5

The Equation

I turned 35 years old in 1968, and while I felt
great and had as much enthusiasm as ever for
bowling, things weren't going right for me.
I denied it at the time, but looking back it
seems obvious that age was a factor in my
difficulties. Top athletes in any sport begin
to lose their physical "edge" in their middle
30s. Bowling isn't a reaction sport like baseball or basketball, and it doesn't require the
man-against-man strength of football. But in
a way it's tougher than those sports, because
we touring professionals are out there day
after day, with no teammates to fall back on,
and we have a lot of time to think and chew
our nails while we're competing. The mental-
stress side of bowling takes more out of you
than most people realize.

I guess, too, that turning 35 was a psychological problem for me. Before that, I'd
always been a kid in my own mind, the boy

wonder of my early days in the Classic League, moving up on the old timers ahead of me on the ladder. Now—and suddenly, it seemed—I was older than most of the guys I was bowling against, and the fact that I'd been around so long made me even more of a graybeard in their eyes. I was only a kid in the sense that I was kidding myself when I thought I could turn back the clock.

But something else was happening at that time that I think had more to do with my problems than any personal midlife crisis: The condition of the lanes had changed.

People who bowl in one league for recreation, or who follow professional bowling only occasionally, probably write off as sour grapes the pros' complaints about lane conditions. Golf pros gripe about any course on which they can't shoot a 66 with six clubs in their bags, and the sun is always getting into some outfielder's eyes. Alibis are as important to athletes as their jockstraps. But in the case of the PBA tour, where the difference in ability from the top of the prize-money list to the bottom is maybe five percent, lane conditions really are an important factor in determining who wins and who doesn't.

The conditions of a lane can shift from one day to the next because of the way the maintenance man oils it. Every bowler who travels knows this. What happened in the late 1960s went beyond that. The basic lane surface—the material *under* the oil—was changed.

When I started bowling, just about every lane in Chicago was coated with shellac. This is a soft finish that slows a hard-thrown ball and grabs its rotational motion, allowing it to hook. A lot of bowlers in that era threw big hooks, but mine was exceptional. My exaggerated release produced the kind of big-bellied curve that later would have stamped me as a "cranker," like Mark Roth is today. Not only did my ball move in a wide arc, but it had great energy. If I could steer it to the head pin, its rotary action would cause terrific destruction. I used to like to say that it "demoralized" the pins.

The key to my delivery was a violent wrist turn. I spun the ball so fast that when someone would put a bit of tape on it to observe the action, the tape would blur. My delivery wasn't pretty, but it was effective. *Bowlers Journal* magazine called mine the "most physical" game on the early PBA tour.

Lane coatings during the 1950s and early 1960s changed from shellac to lacquer or a product called Mineralastic. Neither were quite as soft as shellac, but the difference wasn't great. The change that almost killed me was the one to polyurethane plastic finishes that began in the middle 1960s and had reached the majority of the major bowling centers by the last years of that decade. Polyurethane was adopted partly because it was much easier to maintain than shellacs or lacquers, which accumulated grit and had to be stripped off and replaced fairly frequently. Proprietors also turned to it because it wasn't flammable, and, thus, held down their insurance costs. I understand that in some cities, the fire laws now require polyurethane coatings for all bowling lanes.

When I threw my big hook on a polyurethane lane, especially one that had been oiled fairly heavily, it would slide and skitter. There was nothing for it to grab onto. The best analogy I can think of is an auto trying to get traction on an icy street. I was spinning my wheels, and the tow truck was nowhere in sight.

I wasn't the only bowler in trouble at that time. Several other of the big hookers of the 1950s and 1960s, most notably Ray Bluth, Harry Smith, Billy Welu and Glenn Allison, also found that their games had become obsolete. They pretty much packed it in after the change to polyurethane became permanent, although age and waning enthusiasm also might have played a role. That didn't make it easier for me, though. Bowling had been my life for so long that I couldn't— wouldn't—entertain the idea of giving it up.

As my meager money-winnings figure that year showed, things began to get bad for me in 1968. The next year was worse, even though my tour earnings rose by about $1,000 to just over $13,000. I went six straight tournaments without cashing that year, my longest streak of that sort. And when I did manage to cash, it usually was at the bottom end of the list, for $1,000 or less. For a man 36 years old with heavy travel expenses and a wife and daughter to support (Corinne was born in 1956), that wasn't a living wage.

I did a lot of things to try and get back on the track, all without success. I dug up films of me bowling in my earlier days, when I was winning, to see if I could detect any changes in my style. The major thing I noticed was that I had more hair when I was younger, hardly a revelation.

I looked at just about every new ball on the market to see if any of them could straighten me out. I put one ball in an oven to soften it, but only succeeded in melting it out of shape and smelling up my apartment. Another time I poured a plastic solution into my finger holes to improve my grip. When I placed the ball to dry near a hot plate in my hotel room, the damned thing caught fire.

I changed my diet, buying a blender and juice extractor and making fruit or vegetable cocktails wherever I went. Jim Stefanich, my usual roommate on the tour, finally couldn't take it any more and moved out. I couldn't blame him. Our hotel rooms looked like a garden, with oranges, lemons, grapefruit, carrots, celery, beets and tomatoes all over the place. Stefanich said that if I kept eating that stuff, I'd sprout long ears, like Bugs Bunny.

The PBA tour is a small world, and the other players knew all about my problems. Some of them tried to help by offering advice, but, of course, they only succeeded in confusing me. I got tired of getting sympathy from my friends and smirks from my enemies, and began to withdraw. I'd go out and bowl, then retreat to my hotel room to contemplate my failures in private. I was depressed a lot, and snappish with the people around me. They started avoiding me, which increased my isolation. After bombing out of one tourney after the first qualifying round, I locked myself in my hotel room for five solid days, phoning only Ginny to let her know where I was.

The word around the tour, expressed in subtle and unsubtle ways, was that I was washed up. Once, during a tournament in Tucson, Arizona, I walked by the cocktail lounge in the bowling center and heard a tableful of bowlers talking about me.

"Poor Carmen's having an awful time," said one.

"Ah, he's an old man. What do you expect?" said another.

"He's just making a fool of himself. He ought to go home," said a third.

I looked into the place to see who those guys were. They looked back at me. They were embarrassed, and I was angry. No words passed between us, but I made a point of remembering who had said what. I thought to myself, "You guys can talk now, but I'll retire all of you."

I needed a friend and a guide, and I found both in Hank Lahr. I'd known Hank from my earliest days in the Classic

League. We met first, I think, at Marigold Bowl, where we bowled a match for a few dollars. He won, and I invited him to Schueneman & Flynn's for a rematch. I was mostly kidding, because everyone around Chicago knew by then that I was unbeatable at S & F, but Hank took me up on it. I beat him there, but the fact that he accepted my challenge impressed me mightily. We bowled doubles together after that, and made a pretty good team against some of the best players around.

Hank was 11 years older than I, but we got to be good friends. The more I knew him, the more I respected him. He'd been born in Alsace-Lorraine, where Germany and France meet, and had come to the United States as a child with his parents. He was an engineer by profession and a bowler by passion. He liked to say that the game's angles, spins, and speeds appealed to his mind, and the crash of the pins to his soul. He was a square-built, powerful man, with big hands, long arms and a broad upper body that was a bit out of proportion to the rest of him. His nickname, "The Bear," pretty well describes his physique.

For the first 10 or so years of our acquaintance, Hank couldn't decide whether his bowling or his engineering came first. For awhile, he had an engineering job by day and bowled professionally at night. We were teammates on the Chez Paree team that won the championship of the North End Traveling League in 1959. My 211 average led the league that season, and Hank was close behind at 209. In late 1961 and early 1962, he bowled full time with the San Antonio team in the NBL. That was one of the first teams to fold, and the experience helped sour him on a life as a traveling pro.

I think, though, that what really decided Hank against making a living on the lanes was that he didn't want to devote all his time to a single, narrow subject. Hank had wide-ranging interests and a depth of knowledge that never failed to amaze me. He could talk about physics and mathematics, philosophy and semantics. If you wanted to know the chemistry of some material, Hank could tell you. If the subject was tiddly winks, he'd know all about that, too.

But he still loved bowling so much that he was a familiar figure around the lanes even after he'd finally cast his lot with engineering. One time Hank had to break off a match with Oscar Stevenson, the guy who stuck his head through a ball-return hoop in that crazy match with me, because he had an early business appointment the next morning, but he promised Oscar that he'd renew the competition any time he was free. At about four o'clock the next Saturday morning, Hank was asleep at home when his telephone rang. "It's me, Oscar," said the voice on the other end. "You're not working now, so get over here to Marigold and bowl me." And that was just what Hank did.

I picked Hank to help me after that horrible 1969 season because he knew bowling thoroughly and was someone I could trust and confide in. It isn't easy for an athlete who has been on top to go to someone for help. You've got to have a very strong ego to succeed in sports, and, as you've probably gathered by now, mine was as strong as any. Most athletes would rather follow the old saw about sticking with the style that "brung" them than start experimenting with new approaches that might make them look awkward, even for a short time. But I had done so poorly for so long that it was obvious I had to change or quit. And, I must say, I was looking forward to the challenge of seeing if I could get back on top, something that very, very few athletes have done.

Hank made it easy for me by offering, immediately and without strings, as much time as I might need. That was what friends are for, he said. He told me that another reason he welcomed the chance to help me was that he'd been thinking about bowling and bowlers for a long time, and had some theories he was anxious to put to the test.

He also made clear what our relationship would be during his tutorship. "You may be the big-time pro, but I'm going to be the teacher here, and you're going to be the student," he said. "I don't want you taking a little of what I tell you and mixing it with other people's advice and who knows what else. It won't work unless you stick with me one hundred percent.

"It's going to take time, and it's going to get complicated," Hank went on. "I'll be using words you won't understand at first. It's going to require a kind of effort you've never had to make. But I promise you, if you 'graduate,' you'll bowl better than you ever have."

I said okay; after all, what did I have to lose? If I'd have been doing well, I wouldn't be needing advice in the first place. Also, I'd just read the most remarkable thing about Andy Varipapa, one of the greatest bowlers of all time. Andy had been suffering from right arm and wrist problems, and hadn't bowled in several years. But in that year, 1970, at the age of 78, he'd taken up bowling left-handed, and was doing pretty well! I thought that if a 78-year-old man could start again from scratch, what I was about to do wouldn't be all that difficult.

I'd known Andy only slightly at that time. He was a New

Yorker while I was from Chicago, and he'd reached his bowling peak in the middle 1940s, before I'd hit the big time. But we'd been introduced, and he'd taken a liking to me. "We're both Italian," he'd say with a laugh, "so we gotta stick together."

Right away, Andy gave me a nickname: "Number Two." He'd say, "I'm the number one Italian bowler, and you're number two."

"Anything you say, Andy," I'd reply. I mean, I'd read about this guy since I was little, and I knew how, at age 55, he'd won the grueling All-Star tournament in Chicago in 1946. That was one of the greatest feats ever in bowling. And there he was, with his arm around me, treating me as his equal. Or almost.

Later on, I got to know Andy better. We both were elected to membership in the Italian-American Sports Hall of Fame in Chicago, and when he'd come into town for the annual dinners, I'd meet him at the airport, take him to his hotel, and chauffeur him around town. Even well into his 80s, he was strong and quick of mind. I remember I was taking him someplace in my car once, and couldn't find an address. He told me to move over and let him drive. I did, and he drove right to the place, even though it had been a long time since he'd spent more than a few days a year in Chicago. That was one amazing guy, and his example always inspired me.

So I told Hank Lahr that I was signing on. "Let's get started," I said. "Let's go bowling."

That, however, wasn't what Hank hand in mind. "We're not going bowling," he said. "We're going to *talk* about bowling. Until now, you've been performing instinctively, like a typical jock. I don't want you to pick up a ball until you understand why you've been doing poorly and what it will take for you to make things right again. We're going to talk about translational and rotational motion, and vector analysis. You are going to understand the principles of friction. We're going to attack bowling the way a couple of scientists would. You're going to *be* a scientist.''

For the first few weeks, Hank refused to meet me in a bowling center. We'd meet at his or my home, or in a restaurant. And we'd talk. And talk. I knew something about physical stress, but the mental stress of those conversations was new. At first, I'd get headaches after three or four hours. It would feel like someone was putting a big rubber band around my forehead and turning it tight. The more we talked, though, the more I could handle. Some weekends we'd get together at eight or nine o'clock in the morning and keep at it until past midnight. Slowly but surely, I was getting the message.

The message was this: Every action I took with my ball affected its course. I had to take apart my delivery piece by piece and identify what motion produced what reaction. Only by recognizing the cause could I understand the effect.

Hank broke down bowling to a mathematical equation, which could be stated simply. He said that E-total was total energy; ET was the energy of translational forces; ER was the energy of rotational forces, and ELF was energy loss caused by lane friction. E-total equalled ET plus ER minus ELF.

The bowler's arm swing produced ET, the translational force that propelled the ball down the lane. The bowler's wrist turn produced ER, the rotation that made the ball spin and change direction, or hook. Friction was a function of the moving ball interacting with a lane's underlying coating and surface oil.

That was "The Equation" that all the bowling magazines made such a fuss over after I'd made my comeback. I'd put them up to it by whispering it around and making it mysterious, knowing full well that writers couldn't resist trying to expose a secret. The fact, of course, was that the equation was a way of thinking about bowling scientifically, not a way to knock down pins. Once Hank explained it to me so that I understood it, and could translate it into physical actions, the real work began.

Hank and I would sit down with pencil and paper and work out hypothetical bowling situations. If I threw a ball this hard, with this much wrist turn, on this type of surface, what would happen? What would happen if I turned my wrist, say, from six o'clock to two o'clock instead of from six o'clock to one o'clock? Now, let's say that the lane was more oily. How would that influence the speed with which I should throw the ball, or the amount of wrist turn? How about a drier lane?

Lahr delivered other opinions about bowling that helped reshape my attitude and, eventually, my game. He said there was no such thing as luck in bowling, because the balls and pins always behave in strict conformity with physical laws. He said to forget about how one looked on the lanes as long as one's fundamentals were correct, and concentrate on what knocked down the most pins. He fully endorsed golfer Sam Snead's famous motto, "Nobody asks how, just how many." I quickly came to agree with him on those points.

I recognized before I started that I would have to slow down my ball in order to control it better. Hank and I set ourselves to figuring out in our minds how to do this before we tried it out in practice. Again, we proceeded from the mental to the physical. I think the fact that I was able to put into almost immediate use the changes we worked out attests to the wisdom of that approach.

The changes had the overall effect of making my delivery simpler and more compact. Where I used to hold the ball high in front of me with both hands to start, Hank suggested I hold it in my right hand only and allow it to dangle straight down my right side. I went from a five-step approach to four steps. I reduced my backswing from above my shoulder to below it. My stroke became more even and classic, although that was not our main intent. Reducing my arm swing automatically reduced the speed of my wrist turn, and took the belly out of my hook. I still hooked, only the curve covered five or six boards instead of the previous eight or ten. More important, I could control my ball better, which allowed me to compensate more easily for variations in lane conditions. What I did was similar to what Jim Kaat, the former Major League baseball pitcher, did when he switched from a windup to a no-windup delivery. Kaat had some of his best years after he did that, and so would I.

I altered some things besides my delivery. Where I once worked my way into a tournament by using my practice rounds to figure out the lane conditions, I began arriving at tourney sites a day early. I'd look closely at the lanes, and then go back to my hotel and do some calculations to try to determine what arm speed and wrist turn might produce the best results. That often helped me get a better start on the score board. (Here I should note that PBA bowlers aren't allowed to crawl around on the lanes before a tourney like golfers can on their greens. We have to check things out by eye or observing the oil rings that stick to our bowling balls during practice. That's a tougher proposition by far.)

The other thing I changed was the way I practiced. Rather than just go out and try to knock down pins before tournaments, I'd experiment with the speed and spin calculations I'd worked out in my hotel beforehand. Putting tape on my bowling balls to see how they behaved was something I did occasionally before my lessons from Hank, but I did it constantly afterward in practice. My tournament preparation became better than it had been, and eventually this reflected itself in improved finishes.

I put my new style on display in late 1971 and determined to stick with it no matter what the early results. It turned out that I could bowl fairly well that way from the outset. I had averaged between 205 and 210 in my last good years as a cranker, and was only 10 or 12 pins below those figures after my first few months with a more-compact delivery. Ten or twelve pins is a lot when you're bowling against the best in the world, though, and I had to scratch to make expenses. My tour earnings in 1970 rose to $18,053 and to $19,380 in 1971. But I won no major tournaments in either year, and rarely made my way into the top dozen places in any tour event.

The year 1972 was an off-and-on one for me. My PBA winnings sank to $16,135, which was discouraging. But in a couple of non-PBA tournaments, I showed some of my old flash. One was the ABC Classic Doubles in Long Beach, California, which I won with Barry Asher. I have to admit that Asher kind of carried me in that one. His three-game score was 719 to my 647. But I felt I'd made a solid contribution to the victory, and it was great being back on top in a major event. Showing I could win again gave me the encouragement I needed to keep plugging with my new style.

It was ironic that Barry Asher was instrumental in my return to form, because just a few years later this very talented bowler would have a performance crisis that would end his career prematurely. Barry came on the tour in the late 1960s with one of the most powerful games I've ever seen. We used to compare his "fastball" with that of Sandy Koufax, the great Los Angeles Dodger baseball pitcher. In fairly short order, he won 10 PBA titles, a figure that few have matched.

But then Barry developed a problem that made it tough for him to bowl in tournaments or, even, league play. He would stand on an approach, holding his ball, and his feet would refuse to move. Often, he'd have to sit down and start again, throwing on the run to avoid a set position. Eventually, even the prospect of bowling would trigger his freeze reaction, and when he could fight it no longer, he quit. I'd seen a similar thing happen 10 years earlier to Morrie Oppenheim, one of my mates on the Munsingwear team in the Chicago Classic League, and with the same result. It's nerves, not anything physical. Asher was fine when he wasn't bowling, and the last I heard he was doing great in business in California, where he's from.

In September of 1972, I finished second to Johnny Petraglia in the Bellows-Valvair Open in Painesville, Ohio. The next month I went to Japan to play in the Gold Cup, an annual tournament they started a few years after Carter and I broke the ice with our 1962 visit. I averaged 223 to lead the field through the 54-game qualifying rounds, but lost in the finals when Asher threw a last-frame strike to edge me, 248-237. Still, it was my best showing since my change of style.

My long-awaited breakthrough victory on the tour came at the 1973 Lincoln-Mercury Open in New Orleans. I correctly diagnosed the oily lane conditions at Pelican Bowl and led the tournament through its early rounds. Then the lanes turned drier and my calculations went awry. I barely made the fifth and last spot in the televised final round on Saturday.

Lahr always encouraged me to work things out on my own, and usually I did, but the night before the New Orleans rolloff I phoned him at home in Chicago to discuss ways to deal with the new lane conditions. Actually, I did the proposing, and he kind of uh-huhed me along, confirming my calculations when they were correct and suggesting a point or two that hadn't occurred to me. The conversation was more to give me reassurance than to change the way I had been thinking. I went out on the lanes the next day with more confidence than I'd felt in years. I beat the fourth-place finisher, Dennis Swayda, 225-183; the third-placer, Gus Lampo, 248-212; and the second-placer, Alex Seymour, 236-216. In the final I strung five straight strikes to wipe out Bob Strampe, 245-204. My prizes included $10,000 and a new car.

I went through the usual press interviews afterward, and in the course of answering questions revealed my phone call to Hank the night before. "Hey, you dialed a win!" said one reporter. "Yeah, dial-a-win," I laughed. That became my new gimmick. When people would ask me why I was doing well again, I'd tell them that all I had to do was dial a telephone number and my genius-adviser would give me an instant formula for victory.

For the next seven years—1973 through 1979—I did

some of the best bowling of my life, winning seven PBA tour events and averaging $37,000 a year in official prize money. In 1975 I won the Showboat Invitational tournament in Las Vegas and a $14,000 first prize, the second-largest on the circuit that year. My total 1975 prize money came to $52,483, good for third place behind Earl Anthony and Dave Davis. *Bowlers Journal* named me to its All-American first team. I won $45,290 in 1976 and was named a first-team All-American by *Bowling Magazine,* which had put me on its second team in 1963, '67 and '73. In case your math is rusty, let me remind you that I turned 40 years of age in 1973, when my comeback began. There's nothing like seeing your name in the sports-page headlines to ease the transition to your forties.

My schooling by, and friendship with, Hank Lahr did more than make me a winner again in my sport. It opened my eyes to a whole new way of looking at things, and brought to the surface some talents I never suspected I had. Instead of being a spectator of the world, I became an analyst, probing for the reasons behind things. My starting point was bowling; specifically, bowling balls and their construction.

Each ball has a weight block composed of a heavy material that is supposed to restore the balance lost by the sphere when material is removed in the drilling of the thumb and finger holes. The weight block usually is a single, pancake-shaped mass situated between the holes, thicker in the center than at the outer rim. Like most experienced bowlers, however, I knew from observation that balls really *weren't* balanced, because they would wobble on the lanes or otherwise exhibit rolling patterns that were less than stable. Yet when we weighed them on standard, counter-weight scales, they came up balanced.

I thought about this for awhile, and it occurred to me that while the balls might appear to be in balance in a *static* state, they were out of balance dynamically, which is to say when they are in use. It's like putting a carpenter's bubble on top of an automobile that's standing still, and another on one that's in motion. The trouble was that no device existed to measure the dynamic balance of a bowling ball.

On my own time, with Ginny's help, I started drilling out the weight block material in bowling balls and experimented with replacing it in different places. It was strictly trial and error, and very slow. Once we'd cooked up a ball, I'd take it to the lanes to see how it would perform. If the ball wasn't stable, we'd plug the holes and start again.

In 1979, after six years of experimenting, I solved the balance problem with a system of two weight blocks, one where the thumb hole is drilled and the other where the finger holes go. It sounds simple, but it wasn't. I took my findings to a major bowling-ball manufacturer, and Dr. Thomas Kicher, professor and chairman of the department of mechanical and aerospace engineering at Case-Western Reserve University in Cleveland, who was a consultant for the company, collaborated with me in the testing and evaluation of my two-piece weight block concept. The mathematical formulation for the scheme filled a fat sheaf of papers. I applied for and received a United States patent for my design.

Even though highly qualified academically, Dr. Kicher has the ability not only to relate to the "real world," but also to take laymen's ideas and transfer them into mathematics. I feel fortunate that my friendship with this talented man grew beyond our working association. He professed amazement that I was able to accomplish what I did with no formal scientific training. He said I was like the scientists before Newton, who knew how things worked intuitively, but didn't have the mathematical tools to express their notions precisely.

Bowling balls utilizing my weight-block design appeared on the market, but problems with the cover stock, which had been formulated by the manufacturer, led to their removal after two years. That was a major disappointment for me, but it was cushioned by the excellent response from both professional and amateur bowlers to the rolling characteristics of the ball. I became more determined than ever to see the project through to a better conclusion. I embarked on the study of chemistry so I would have a better understanding of the total makeup of a bowling ball. To those who asked me what I knew about chemistry, I'd say, "You don't have to have the title of 'chemist,' to solve a chemical problem."

It took me three years in the libraries to acquire the background I needed to attack the problems of bowling ball construction and friction. Using a dictionary of terms used in chemistry, I'd sit down with an article or book and read and reread it until I thought I understood it. Then I'd look at the bibliography and pursue the tangents of the subject. I taught myself to crawl, and then to walk. That's a lot harder to do as an adult than as a kid.

When I thought I had a handle on making a ball that would be durable and have better performance characteristics than those available, I again sought professional assistance. I was fortunate that Amoco Research Center in Naperville, Illinois, was just then looking into producing a material for bowling balls. Together with chemist Dan Edwards of Amoco, I customized a new material that has excellent performance characteristics. A similar collaboration between me and Dr. Art Jonas, who is recognized as one of the top chemists in the field of urethane plastics, produced a high-quality ball in that material.

Shortly after completing these two projects, I contacted Tom Malloy, president of the Ebonite Company, and I'm presently under contract as a consultant to their vice president of research and development, Andy Lee. We are working to produce these bowling balls, which Ebonite will call the "Thunderbolt." They already may be on the market as you read this.

There's no doubt that the hours I've devoted to research, especially over the last six or seven years, have hurt my performance on the PBA tour. More than a few times I've gotten so wrapped up in my lab work that I've skipped tournaments I'd intended to bowl, and it has been tough concentrating on bowling with a head full of technology.

For the foreseeable future, though, I'm committed to staying on the tour at my present rate of about 15 tournaments a year. The prospect of bowling with a ball that incorporates the technology I brought to Ebonite is exciting to me, and should keep my interest keen for many years.

My new, inquisitive nature also has paid some unexpected dividends on the home front. My daughter, Corinne, was doing some college math homework, and left her notebook open where I could see it. I gave her figures a quick scan and told her I thought they were wrong. "Oh, Daddy!" she said, like she does when she thinks I'm some relic from the Dark Ages. But I insisted, and she went back and rechecked her calculations. It blew her mind when she discovered that her old man was right. From that day on, she has had a better respect for my intellect, although she still argues with me.

Being with Hank put other facets of my life into new perspective. I read more than I used to, and I've expanded my circle of friends beyond the narrow confines of sports. I'm more willing to try new things and I've stopped being surprised at how much pleasure I find when I come across something that expands my horizons.

I've developed a habit of never putting a new question out of my mind. When someone asks me something I don't know, and the question isn't trivial, I try never to say, simply, "I don't know." I say, "I don't know *at this time*." Saying "I don't know" implies "I don't care," that my ignorance on a subject is permanent. I try to file away those questions and learn the answers, even if I never again expect to see the persons who asked them.

I've come to define success not in terms of winning or losing, or meeting other people's expectations, but by how I perform relative to my own capacities. If I feel I have done my best in a tournament, or a relationship, I consider it to be successful no matter how it turns out. There are things a person can control and things he can't, and there's no use worrying about the latter.

Similarly, I've abandoned the notion of having goals in life, except for the general one of working as hard as I can in every situation to which I commit myself. When you select a specific goal—say, to win three tournaments in a year, or $100,000 in prize money—you put a ceiling on your expectations. I want everything to be wide open because I want to know everything. Putting on blinders in pursuit of specific aims shuts you out of a good deal that's worthwhile in life.

I've come to believe that attitude and adjustment are more important to success in sports, or any field, than another "a" word, aptitude. The difference between competitors on the

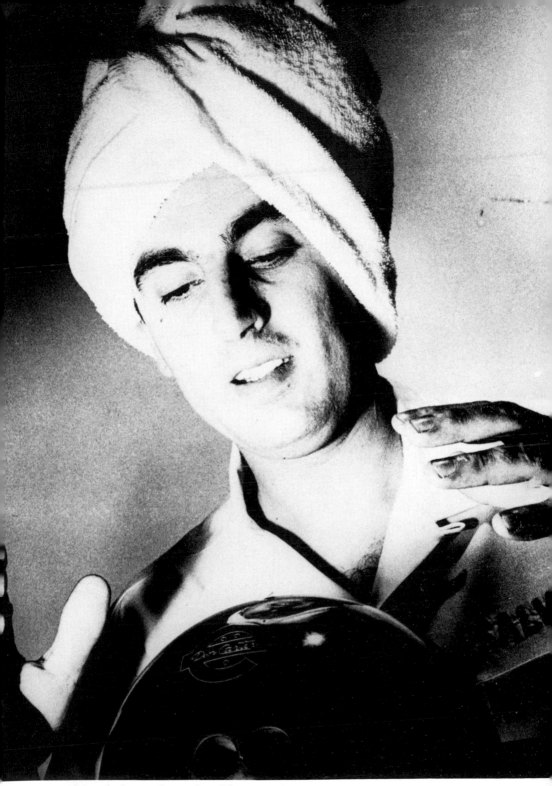

If I only knew then what I know now.

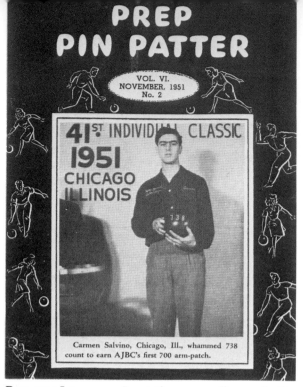

PREP PIN PATTER

VOL. VI.
NOVEMBER, 1951
No. 2

41ST INDIVIDUAL CLASSIC
1951
CHICAGO
ILLINOIS

Carmen Salvino, Chicago, Ill., whammed 738 count to earn AJBC's first 700 arm-patch.

Boy, was I nervous. I put the wrong fingers in the ball.

Me and the Delneros gang forty years ago. My first team. Great outfits—especially the shoes!

1955
B.P.A.A.
National Doubles
CHAMPIONSHIP

The most gentle man I ever bowled with, Joe Wilman.

Where have all the years gone? This was Alcazar Hotel, my first pro team, in 1952. Top Row, left to right: John Giovanelli, Me, Ray Blank. Bottom Row, left to right: Bill White, Les Kilbourne, Rudy Hazuka.

Me, Joe Wilman and Art Butler. The president of Tri-Par Radio just signed the check, and we needed the money.

●

We didn't smile that much after we bowled. Me, Ed Kawolics, Paul Krumske, Earl Johnson and Chuck Hamilton, of the Peter Hands Beer team, 1957.

●

AMERICAN BOWLING CONGRESS

FORT WORTH 1957

I'm grateful I never had to make a living singing.
Me, Pat Patterson and Hank Lahr. Conductor—
unknown.

●

You can see that I have my hands full—talk to me
later. The Chez Paree Adorables. Also (bottom
row), Ace Calder, Mo Miller, Hank Lahr, Ray
Shannon and Tony Gardini.

●

It figures, the guy with the ball is the captain.
Chuck Wagner, Harry Ledene, Jr., Art Butler, Joe
Norris, Me and Joe Wilman. The Hamm's Beer
team, 1954.

●

I'm not too sure about the outcome.

Maybe I should have been a high jumper.

Ginny and Carmen—true love.

Quit posing for the camera and roll the ball.
Daughter Corinne and me.

How many times have I told you, kid, stay behind
the foul line. You better get a job, 'cause you're not
going to make it.

You can see that the hair is starting to go. It's 1962.

OK, Hank Marino, I'll follow through higher.

The Kim Sisters—and they could bowl too—with Don Carter and me.

In Japan in 1962, third from left, Don Carter, and next to him the greatest host and nicest gentleman I ever bowled for, Tom Horiike.

With a little more belly I could be a Suma wrestler.
Me, Geisha girl and Les Schissler.

Geisha girl and me; when in Tokyo, do as the Japanese do.

A great team captain, Buddy Bomar (far left), and well known Chicago radio personality, Sam Weinstein, The Ten Pin Tattler.

The first "no wind-up" delivery in bowling.

The Greatest, Andy Varipapa, with No. 2.

The two most beautiful women in the world, Ginny and daughter Corinne. Induction into the ABC Hall of Fame, 1979.

Chicago Sports Hall of Fame legends. Stan Mikita, Me, George Ireland, Sid Luckman and Ray Meyer.

One king to another, both Chicago Match Game Kings. Ed Kawolics and Me.

Me, Tom Lasorda and Ginny. If I had his gift of gab, I'd be a millionaire like him.

The most memorable picture I've had the honor to be in.

National Italian American Sports Hall of Fame
Tenth Anniversary January 17th, 1987

Top Row—L-R—Carmen Basilio, Alex DelVecchio, Charlie Trippi, Vic Raschi, Lou Duva, Joe Torre, Dan Marino, Founder George F
Daryl LaMonica, Tony Esposito, Dominic DiMaggio, Leo Nomellini, Gino Cappelletti.
Bottom Row—L-R—Tony DeMarco, Joey Maxim, Joey Giardello, Willie Mosconi, Carmen Salvino, Donna Caponi, Joe Di
Jean Carnera Hamilton, Jake LaMotta, Rocky Graziano, Dante Lavelli, Andy Robustelli.

professional bowling tour isn't a function of talent. Every guy out there has that. The winners—Don Carter, Dick Weber, Earl Anthony, Mark Roth and Carmen Salvino—win because they want to win, have the brains to recognize changing conditions, and the flexibility to adjust to those changes. They didn't allow their minds to get lazy, or to put *looking* good ahead of *doing* good. Hank Lahr taught me that.

Hank died in 1980 at the age of 58—far too early. By opening my mind to life's possibilities, he gave me the greatest gift anyone can bestow. His memory will live at least as long as I do.

6

The Modern Tour

Turning points always look clear-cut in the history books, but when you're living through one it's anything but. People often ask me when the modern era on the PBA tour started, and I really don't know what to tell them. It all depends on what you want to use as your frame of reference.

If it's lane technology you're talking about, it began with that late-1960s switch to polyurethane from lacquer or Mineralastic as the dominant undercoating. If it's bowling ball technology, you probably have to move into the early 1970s, when ball manufacturers began tinkering seriously with hardness and friction compounds and bowlers realized that a ball could be more than round and black.

The changing of the players' guard, I think, dates from 1975, when Earl Anthony, the tall left-hander from Tacoma, Washington, became the first man to win more than

$100,000 in a single year on the PBA tour, and firmly established himself as the game's leading light. Dick Weber, who had dominated the tour in the 1960s, had passed his prime by that point, even though he had some wins left in him, and so had guys like Ray Bluth, Harry Smith, Dick Hoover and Bob Strampe, whose roots went back with mine to the Big Team days.

Me? Like I said before, I had some juice left. I had my biggest money-winning year in 1975 and won tournaments in '76, '77, '79 and '84. But by the later years of the 1970s, Mark Roth and Marshall Holman had joined Anthony in pushing aside the old-timers as the most frequent occupants of the winner's circle.

One thing that certainly changed in 1975 was the competitive atmosphere of the tour. Anthony's $100,000-plus year (his actual winnings came to $107,585) put out the word that it was possible to make a decent living as a professional bowler, and the number of guys trying to do that shot upward. Not only did the quantity of players vying for spots in our tournaments increase, but so did the quality. Through the early 1970s, maybe 15 or 20 bowlers stood a real chance of winning a tour event in any given week. By the last years of that decade, the figure had climbed to close to 50.

In fact, though, bowling hasn't become the dollar bonanza for its players that golf and tennis have, and the frustration of some members over money problems has been a growing source of friction within the PBA. During my tenure as president in 1985 and 1986, the PBA was sued by a group of members who wanted to change its rules to allow them to play in exhibitions whose dates and places conflicted with official tour events, and negotiate endorsements in conflict with PBA efforts in that area. The PBA contested the suit, and I firmly believe that the rules then extant were in the best interest of most of the members. I sympathized with the desire of the bowlers to expand their money-making opportunities, but I thought they should try to find solutions inside the "family."

A look at the 1986 prize-money lists in the individual sports of bowling, golf and tennis illustrates the different depths of the three sports' prize pools. Walter Ray Williams, Jr., led the PBA with $145,550 in winnings that year and three other bowlers—Holman, Steve Cook and Dave Husted—earned $100,000 or more. Twenty-eight bowlers topped the $50,000 mark in prize money, which is about the minimum it takes to come out ahead on the tour in these days of high travel expenses.

By contrast, Greg Norman led the golf pros in 1986 official winnings with $653,296. Eighty-three members of the Professional Golfers Association earned $100,000 or more, and 136 players topped the $50,000 mark. In tennis, Ivan Lendl led at $1,987,537. Fifty-five players earned $100,000 or more, and more than 100 took home more than $50,000.

The main reason that the golfers and tennis players make so much more money than we bowlers is that they routinely play before paying crowds of up to 20,000 a day, while daily attendance at our tournaments rarely exceeds 2,000. Gate receipts are such a miniscule part of the financial picture of the PBA tour that they aren't part of the purse structure, which comes entirely from television and sponsorship revenues.

There have been attempts to put the finals of PBA events in arenas or auditoriums with good-sized seating capacities. About 6,000 people paid to see the last few rounds of a tournament in Mobile, Alabama, 15 or so years ago, and a New

York tourney once wound up in the Felt Forum section of Madison Square Garden before a similar sized crowd. Proprietors of a few events in regular bowling centers have used movable bleachers to pack in a few hundred more spectators for their Saturday finals. For the present, however, the expense and difficulties of installing portable lanes in sports arenas for what can't be more than a one-day show (our fields are too large to go into an arena before our five-player roll-offs) precludes our cracking the attendance barrier in any real way. The fact that we've been able to increase purses at all in recent years is a tribute to the abilities of Eddie Elias and Commissioner Joe Antenora in negotiating with the sponsors and television networks.

For some players, including some exceptional ones, the economics of the tour don't work out favorably. Mike Durbin, who had won 14 tour events and more than $700,000 in prize money, dropped out to run a bowling center a couple years ago because he preferred a steady income to the vicissitudes of bowling for prize money, and later went to work for the PBA. Less-accomplished bowlers play the tour for a few months, go home to replenish their wallets, and then try their luck again for a few more.

One of the ways that players—especially young married ones—keep expenses down is to tour in mobile homes, and the parking lots of the host bowling centers during tournament week resemble trailer courts. Some of the guys log so many miles behind the wheel during a year that they joke that they're really preparing for the Indianapolis 500. But when you figure what they save on hotels and restaurants, it makes sense.

Another advantage to those big trailers is that they allow players to haul a lot of bowling balls between tournaments.

Some guys travel with as many as 40 balls. That's another big difference between bowling's early days and today's PBA tour. When I turned pro, most players would take one or two balls to a tournament, and a real "ball freak" might take four. Bowling was an art then; every lane was shellacked, and when oil conditions changed you'd vary your speeds, angles or wrist turns to compensate. If you found a ball you liked, you stuck with it. I remember using balls until their covers cracked.

Nowadays, a ball is discarded if it's bruised a bit, or even before that if a new model comes along. The PBA has a rule limiting to eight the number of bowling balls players could take into the locker rooms at tournaments, because otherwise there wouldn't be room for the bowlers to sit. But some guys get around that by getting metal racks that hold a dozen or more balls, keeping them in their vans, and bringing them into the center when they bowl. When lane conditions change, they'll usually change balls instead of adjusting their deliveries.

It's reached the point where some pro bowlers won't endorse any manufacturer's line because they are afraid another manufacturer will come out with a better ball, and they won't be able to use it. Not only will some guys change to different balls if they hear they're better in some way, but they'll also watch the serial numbers that give the month and year a ball was made, and try to get balls from the same *batch* as one that a leader in the previous week's tournament had success with.

In earlier and simpler days, when a player would win a tournament, the other players would say, "Nice shooting. I'll get you next week." Now, after someone wins, the other pros gather around to see what balls he's using. In the tug of war between art and science, science very definitely is winning on the lanes.

(There is, incidentally, no rule limiting the number of balls a player can use as long as he registers each ball with tournament officials and has them checked for balance before and after play. The checking is done so bowlers won't alter their balls in ways that exaggerate their hooking action and increase their "pop" in the pocket. Bowlers have been known to tamper with balls in much the same way that baseball players load their bats with cork or other foreign substances.)

It's my opinion that some guys have taken this bowling-ball thing too far, and anyone who thinks he must use a dozen in a tourney has other problems. I never travel with more than eight, or actually use more than a half-dozen. In part, though, the hang-up is understandable because of the confusion over lane conditions that exists on the tour today.

The trouble started, I think, with that switch to poly-urethane lane coatings in the late 1960s. Poly is okay as far as it goes, but it doesn't absorb oil dressings the way previous lane finishes did, and used with oil it can lead to drastic and rapid changes in conditions from center to center, lane to lane in the same center, or, even, in the same lanes over a few hours. It's a classic example of what can happen when new products overwhelm a sport's (or an industry's) capacity to absorb them properly, no pun intended. Making the situation worse is that research to attain uniformity among the various lane coatings has been slow to develop. Some promising work finally is underway, but as I write this it hasn't borne much fruit.

The BPAA and the ABC have been squabbling over lane conditions as long as I can remember, but the issues involved didn't reach the general sports public until the flap over Glenn

Allison's 900 series in July of 1982. Glenn was a great pro in his day. He's a member of both the ABC and PBA halls of fame, and a regular and strong participant in PBA seniors events. He got his perfect series in a league in California, where he lives. To say that it made news would be like saying that Gary Hart has had a girlfriend or two. Everyone who ever rolled a bowling ball instantly recognized the magnitude of his accomplishment.

The ABC investigates all record applications to determine if they were set fairly. It looked into Allison's and ruled against it on ground that the lanes he bowled were improperly oiled. Specifically, it found that the proprietor had oiled the lanes so as to create "crowns" in their centers that, in effect, steered, or "blocked," balls toward the pockets.

The decision raised a hullabaloo, and I can't say I agreed with it. It would have been justified if everybody in the house was rolling 300 games that night, but only Glenn did it. Three straight 300 games in league play is about the most remarkable thing that ever happened in bowling, and the ABC should have given Glenn the benefit of the doubt. Hey, a 900 series would be tough if someone laid a trough into the pocket. Come the seventh or eighth frame of the third game, you'd be shaking so badly you'd probably miss the trough!

The ABC said that the Allison controversy didn't alter its regulatory stance, but there was no doubt that the decibel level of the debate over lane conditions rose with that incident. Proprietors complained that too much guesswork and judgment went into ABC inspectors' rulings on whether their lanes were legal or not. It culminated in a 1986 ABC rule that permitted proprietors to top-dress their lanes *in any manner* to 26 feet past the foul line as an alternative to even, channel-to-channel dressing over longer distances.

When "short-oil" is used on the tour, it is almost as disruptive as the switch to polyurethane lanes was 15 or so years before. Short-oiled lanes are drier than longer-oiled ones. This slows down everybody's shots, and has brought some of the big-hooking crankers back to the fore at the expense of the classical stylists. Also, recreational bowlers are lofting their shots more to get them past the oil, and throwing harder to get their hooks to work the way they should. As a direct result of that, I think, we've seen more wrist, arm and shoulder injuries in the last couple of years than in the previous five or ten, especially among young bowlers and seniors.

The guy in the middle on the tour is Lon Marshall, the PBA's lane maintenance director. A former touring pro, he goes to each tournament site a couple of weeks in advance and confers with the proprietor about what's to be done to the lanes. The ABC is always looking over his shoulder— figuratively, at least—and so is every guy who is going to bowl that tournament. Lefties like oil to be laid in one way, righties another. Strokers—the guys with the classic deliveries—like oilier lanes than crankers. There are probably six or eight other style classifications in between.

Lane conditioning is partly a political question within the PBA, with each type of bowler—or constituency—demanding an advantage. Marshall varies the conditions from week to week to make almost everybody happy some of the time. Also, he's got to take into consideration the effects of the lane dressing on general scoring. He doesn't want to make the lanes so easy that everyone will be rolling 250s, or so hard that scores of 200 are hard to get. In balance, I think, he usually errs on the side of over-toughness. That's why you'll see Saturday finals in which the winners are posting scores in the 190s or even 180s. People sit at home watching, and wonder what's so wonderful about us pros. The fact is that on lanes where a 190 score wins in a final, your average league bowler might have trouble just keeping his shots out of the gutters.

I'm afraid that all the attention to lane conditions and different kinds of balls has had the additional effect of increasing griping on the tour. Sure, guys would complain in the old days, but it usually was about their injuries, real or imagined, or the problems of balancing a salaried job with getting in as much bowling as they wanted. Now, when someone doesn't "cash" in a tourney—that is, finish in the money—it's always because the lanes weren't oiled right, or somebody else's ball was hooking better than his.

The social aspect of professional bowling changed decisively in the middle 1960s, when the PBA tour replaced team events as the primary support of most bowlers. During the tour's early days, most of us still had team affiliations, and we usually would travel in team groups. That meant you had to split with your teammates whatever prize money you won, but it also meant that you had some emotional and practical support. A guy on your team would warn you about a loose board on a lane at the tourney house, or tell you about a good restaurant he'd been to the last time he was in town. And if one of your teammates would win, you could be certain of a victory party later.

Now, every man is pretty much out for himself. That's okay with me for the most part, because I've always been something of a loner. That's especially true on the tour, where I don't want to be in the position of having to answer to

accusations of letting up on a fellow bowler I'm chummy
with in a match where other guys' paychecks are on the line.
Still, I miss the old-time camaraderie.

Bowlers do group together, of course. Naturally, the
ones with young children and big travel vans wind up being
neighbors in most towns, so they see a lot of one another.
So do guys from the same cities. Other fellows pair off from
time to time to share traveling expenses.

Now that I bowl only 15 or so tournaments a year, I
usually travel alone, but I had my share of roommates before.
One of the most memorable was Pete Tountas, who was born
in Greece before he moved to Northwest Indiana, just east
of Chicago. He was a lanky guy, about six-feet-four-inches
tall, and had a very unusual bowling style. He'd just walk
to the line, stop, and throw his ball. He was so strong, and
had such a long armswing, that he could get away with it.

Pete was like me in that he loved to talk. When he got
excited, which was often, he'd mix Greek words with his
English so people would have a hard time understanding him.
He was tall and had a long nose, like me. In fact, we looked
so much alike that we'd sometimes be taken for brothers.
I remember once, he'd made a date with a stewardess we'd
met on a plane. She came to the center where we were
bowling a week or two later, and walked right over to me,
not him. Ginny was there, and I had some explaining to do
before Pete showed up. I'm not sure she believed me even
then.

Another fellow I roomed with for awhile was John Fitch,
who was from Australia and spent a couple of years on the
tour. I guess I gravitated to the foreign-born players because
they could tell me about people I've never met and places
I'd never been. I guess, too, that I've always been attracted

to unusual people, and John, whom we nicknamed "Captain Kangaroo" because of where he was from, surely was one.

You had to see Fitch to really appreciate him. He stood about six-feet-two-inches tall and weighed about 210 pounds. His physique looked like it was carved out of granite, and in Australia he'd played rugby, which is similar to our football and played without pads. He had some strange ideas about keeping in shape.

"Carmen," he said to me one day, "I need some exercise. How about you and me going outside and fightin' a bit?"

I told him I thought he was crazy; I don't relish fighting anyone, much less somebody with muscles in his earlobes. So out he went by himself, and back he came about an hour later with his clothes a little mussed. "Got my exercise!" he smiled. I could just imagine what his partner in that workout looked like.

For all his muscles, though, Fitch basically was a mild guy. His mother, whom he called "Mum," was bankrolling him on the tour, and he'd have three or four telephone conversations a week with her about how he was doing, which usually wasn't too good. She did most of the talking on those calls, which sometimes lasted a long time considering how much money it cost to call Australia. It was funny, a big guy like that sitting there saying, "Yes, Mum," or "No, Mum," over and over.

Fitch also was one of the world's leading hypochondriacs. Something was always bothering him. Once I was playing cards between blocks in a tournament with Mike Meeks, a representative of the Ebonite Company. "The Captain's bowling badly again," said Meeks. "Think he'll blame it on a headache or a bad back?" I guessed headache and Meeks guessed backache. We bet a dollar on it.

Fitch came along some minutes later, singing the blues as usual. "I really bowled lousy today," he said. "My bad back is acting up again."

Meeks started laughing, and the Captain got a little angry. "Hey, that's not funny," he said. "In fact, I have a headache, too." When I started laughing, he thought we were a couple of ghouls.

The fellow I've traveled with most over the years is Jim Stefanich, a very-different type than Pete or the Captain. Jim is one of the best men who ever rolled a bowling ball, and so quiet that people who don't know him think he's stand-offish. His record includes 13 PBA titles, including the 1967 Firestone Tournament of Champions, and he also won the 1968 BPAA All-Star. He was the Sporting News' player of the year in '68, and is in both the ABC and PBA halls of fame. I'd rank him alongside Ned Day as having one of the smoothest, most classical deliveries of all time.

Jim and I go back more than 25 years to the old Chicago major leagues, and we've traveled together off and on for the last 15 years. He's from Joliet, Illinois, near Chicago, which makes it convenient for us to get together. I suppose we've worn well because my gregariousness gets him invited to more parties, and his quiet nature helps calm me down sometimes when I need it. He has a good sense of humor, and is a serious trainer, like me, so he's not running in and out of our room at all hours of the night. He's an excellent all-around athlete, and might be almost as good a golfer as he is a bowler. In fact, I think that his bowling has suffered because of his attention to golf these past few years, and that he'd be better off putting aside the clubs while he can still make a living on the lanes. On the other hand, he could fool everyone by dropping bowling and starting a whole new career on the senior golf tour one of these days.

Traveling with an experienced, savvy pro like Steffy is an advantage to me because we are able to exchange information about lane conditions and other tournament factors. He notices things that a lot of the younger players don't, and so do I, which means that talking to him is never a waste of time. It doesn't make sense to me to just sit around the locker room or cocktail lounge at the tournament site and yap about the lanes the way some bowlers do. In our business, information is money, and I don't pass it out unless I have a special reason to do so, or get some value in return. It's a different story when Steffy and I face each other in a match, though; we pretend like we're strangers. In fact, I think we each try harder than usual to win so we can needle the other about it later.

The only bone I have to pick with Steffy is that he has this habit of wishing he's somewhere he's not. For instance, we'll be invited to two parties and have to choose one to attend, but all the time we're there he'll be bothering me about what the other party might be like. That drives me nuts. But I'm sure he has a much-longer list of things I do that ticks him off.

Steffy might be quiet, but he has one of the best temperaments for bowling I've seen. When things go wrong for him, as they do for everyone from time to time, he'll sit down with me or someone else he trusts and review his delivery point by point, and then he'll do what it takes to get back on the track. The ability to think and bowl at the same time is rare even among the pros. Jim's capacity for that accounts more than anything else for his splendid record.

Another guy I would put in Jim's mental league is Earl
Anthony, the best bowler on the tour for the decade ending
with his temporary retirement in 1984. There was a man who,
literally, made himself a great bowler, and at a fairly advanced age at that. He was a baseball player as a kid, and
never picked up a bowling ball until, as a 21-year-old clerk
in a wholesale grocery firm in Tacoma, he joined a company
team in a local handicap league. It was fully 10 years later,
in 1970, that he came on the PBA tour.

I remember Earl in his early days on the circuit. He was
a quiet person, and very polite; he called me "Mr. Salvino"
the first time we met, even though I'm only five years older
than he is. His left-handed delivery was kind of awkward,
and his shots didn't have great speed or spin.

The more Earl bowled, though, the better he became.
He developed a degree of repeatability that was unmatched
in my experience. Once he got zeroed in, he could hit the
pocket all day long. That got him into a lot of finals in his
early years, but not many titles. Then he taught himself how
to win, which involves being able to turn on his best efforts
when they counted most. When he got that little bit of "tiger"
going, no one could touch him.

Earl's nickname is "Mr. Machine," which suggests a
mechanical approach to the game, but I think that misses the
point of his greatness. The fact is that Earl is a very subtle
bowler who can vary his speeds, angles and spins to compensate for just about any lane condition. He won 42 PBA
tournaments in 14 years, which is a record and remarkable
enough. When you consider that he did it against the best
competition bowling ever had to offer, and on lanes that
varied from very slick to very dry, it becomes downright
amazing. Earl is a throwback to the best of the bowling

craftsmen from the days when I broke in, guys like Ned Day, Buddy Bomar, Paul Krumske and Joe Wilman. I can't think of a nicer compliment to give someone.

Anthony quit the tour in 1984, at age 46, not because his skills were in decline (he won two tournaments, including the PBA National in Toledo, Ohio, his last year out) but because he was burned out by the subsidiary pressures of the game. That, I think, says a lot about the changed atmosphere around professional bowling, particularly the increased news media attention. In the old days, we'd play three or four national events a year that the press (there were no other "mediums" around then) covered extensively, and local leagues the rest of the time. Now, every event is a national one with some sort of television coverage and press conferences for the leaders after every day's action.

Don't get me wrong, I'm not knocking it. We're only big league to the extent that the newspapers and television stations recognize us as such. If I have a beef about the coverage of our tour, it's that we get too little ink, not too much. Moreover, Earl's relations with the reporters were always excellent in every way. But when he was on top—a period of about 10 years—he was the main focus of attention wherever he went, winner or also-ran, and it just got to be too much. He came back to bowl a limited number of events in 1987, and said he enjoyed them more than his ones before, even though he didn't win. Knowing Earl, though, I don't think that will satisfy him for long. I wouldn't be surprised to see him grinding on the practice lanes again, and showing up on TV Saturday afternoons.

The other two fellows who dominated the tour between 1975 and 1985—Mark Roth and Marshall Holman—were quite different sorts than Anthony. Both had considerably more pure talent than Earl did. They haven't equalled Earl's records because they haven't matched his work discipline or mental attitude, although they're both still young (Roth was 36 in 1987 and Holman was 32) and have time to catch up.

Roth is a cranker whose style reminds me of my own when I was younger. He has great intensity on the lanes, and great self-control. He would have made a terrific hustler in the old days, but who needs to hustle when you can win 32 PBA titles like he had through 1986, and almost $1.2 million in career prize money?

Still, I think Roth would be even better if he took better physical care of himself. He has let his weight go a bit in the last few years, and while he's a lot stronger than his roundish physique suggests, this has had to hurt him. The same, I think, goes for his tendency to withdraw off the lanes, especially from the press. He'd rather be at a hockey game or movie than polishing up his image by talking to a reporter. I can't say that he's lost any tournaments because of that, but it might have cost him some endorsements and appearance fees. And that's a shame, because if you get him one-on-one, he's one of the nicest guys around.

Holman, in turn, is just about the opposite sort from Roth: popular and a charmer off the lanes but undisciplined on them. He'd won 20 tournaments when 1987 began, but the number would have been a lot higher if he had better control of his emotions while he bowled.

Anybody with half an eye could see from the first that Holman had all the ability he'd need to be a big winner. He came out with power and rhythm, and the flamboyancy to be a star. The first time I saw him bowl, I was sitting with Bernie Wise from the Columbia Company. After about three frames, I looked at Bernie and Bernie looked at me. "I think you're reading my mind," Bernie said. "This kid is gonna be something, isn't he?" I just nodded.

The trouble is, when things don't go right for Marshall, he blows his cool. He throws towels or whatever else is handy. Once he threw a rosin bag in the air, and some of the dust hit a woman spectator. Other times he gets a little, shall we say, lewd in his gestures, shaking his butt at the pins and things like that. He's kind of like Jimmy Connors, the tennis player, in that respect. If you go out to dinner with Marshall later, and ask him why he does that stuff, he just shrugs and can't explain. He's even apologetic about it. But the next day he'll go out and do it again. Off the lanes, he's great with the press, and has done a lot of good for bowling.

Among the younger pros, nobody stands out more than Dick Weber's son, Pete. Naturally, I know him from way back, since Dick and I traveled the same circuit for so many years. Two of Dick's other sons, Dick Jr., whom everyone calls Rich, and Johnny, also bowled on the tour. In fact, Rich and my daughter, Corinne, met at the tournaments, and were engaged to be married at one time. People would kid them that they were going to breed the greatest bowlers ever. They broke up after about a year, but they're still friends.

Neither Rich nor Johnny had Petey's talent, though, and they certainly didn't have his cheekiness. I remember one morning when both Dick's family and mine were staying in the same motel, and we'd left our door slightly open for one reason or another. Petey, who was about 10 years old, walked in on Ginny and me, flopped down on our bed, and asked if he could finish a pitcher of orange juice we had on the table. While I poured his juice, he asked me to change the channel on our TV set so he could watch a cartoon. Meanwhile, Dick and his wife, Juanita, were running around, frantic, looking for the kid.

We don't see that much of Petey now that he's grown, but apparently he's still kind of wild. He has struggled with drinking and drug problems these last few years, things that, unfortunately, he shares with other athletes, including some bowlers. It'd be a shame if he let that get the best of him, because he's absolutely loaded with ability. He's got great style, and his hands are so quick that he can adjust his shot at the last split-second if he feels it's not right. I don't know anyone, of any age (Pete was 25 years old in 1987), who can match his concentration. Watch his eyes the next time you see him bowl; they're focused on the pins like a couple of needles. Similarly, there are few around who are better in the clutch. Petey is like Earl Anthony in his best years in that he can raise his game when a title is in sight. Very few bowlers can do that.

Right behind Pete are four other young bowlers who look like they could stay near the top for some years to come: Steve Cook, Mike Aulby, Walter Ray Williams, Jr., and Dave Husted. Cook stands six-feet-seven inches tall and weighs 265 pounds. He's the biggest top-flight pro ever. He's the rare lefty who is versatile enough to bowl as well from the center of a lane as from the left-hand corner, which allows him to adapt to different lane conditions. He's got an even temper and a close-to-sixty percent winning record in his finals appearances.

Aulby is a short guy (5-feet-7), also a lefty, with a smooth delivery—another throwback to the old Classic Leaguers. He's got the talent, and the record (13 PBA titles through 1986), but I'm not sure he has the motivation to stick with professional bowling long enough to compile the record he is capable of attaining.

Williams has a peculiar delivery highlighted by a very high follow-through. It looks like he's throwing horseshoes, and that's no accident: He was a national-champion horseshoe pitcher before he came on the tour. He had a sensational year in 1986, winning three titles and leading the money list. He has the size and strength that it takes to win these days, but whether his stroke will hold up remains to be seen.

Husted is a tall, very strong bowler whose delivery combines the striking power of the cranker with the repeatability of the classical stroker. He's just coming into his own on the tour, and his record through 1986 (four PBA titles) doesn't seem to warrant inclusion in this short list of top young bowlers. But I think he has almost unlimited potential, and a style that will ensure a long and successful future in the game.

My last win on the regular PBA tour came at the Miller High Life Classic in Anaheim, California, in 1979. It was the first tournament of the year, and I remember that I almost didn't make it because a snowstorm in Chicago backed up traffic out of O'Hare Airport something fierce, and eventually closed it. I think I caught the last plane out.

I got out to California in time for the pre-tourney press conference. One of the reporters asked me the usual question about how I could stay on the tour as long as I had (I was 45 years old then). I told him it was simple. "I'm a genius," I said, in my most humble manner. I was trying to get their attention, and did.

"If you're so smart, winning this week should be no problem," the guy retorted.

"I guarantee it," I said.

Everybody was laughing during the exchange, but the brag gave me something to live up to, and I got through the qualifying rounds in third place. On Saturday, the lanes came up ice-slick, about the toughest conditions I'd ever seen in a final. It was obvious after a couple of frames that defensive bowling was the only sensible tactic, and I concentrated on staying clean—that is, not leaving any open frames. My 204 winning score in my first match of the finals, against Ernie Schlegel, turned out to be the best score of any of the eight games bowled that day. I beat a 24-year-old Marshall Holman, 199-166, in the semi-final, and defeated Mike Berlin, 192-170, for the championship.

About a half-hour after the tournament ended, the ABC made my day complete by phoning to tell me that I'd been elected to its Hall of Fame. I said thanks and all that, but I really thought that my record warranted election at least five years earlier. Bowling is better than most other sports in that it allows active competitors into its halls of fame, but it still dragged things out too long to suit me. If an athlete's achievements merit it, I can't see why he must be retired to be honored. Seeing an "immortal" in action would be a kick for the younger players as well as the fans, and you wouldn't get situations like baseball's Roberto Clemente dying in a plane crash and being robbed of experiencing the ultimate honor of a great career.

My bowling-ball research was cutting seriously into my practice time by then, making it tough for me to challenge for titles week in and week out, but the Miller Classic win wasn't my last glory day. The next year, at the PBA Nationals in Sterling Heights, Michigan, I set a tour record for 16 games with a score of 4,015, or an average of 251. It's hard to say why something like that happens. All I know is that for two days, every ball I threw, on every lane, went just where I wanted it to go. My scores for my first, eight-game block were 256, 289, 275, 249, 252, 194, 247 and 298. The next day I came back with 258, 235, 231, 257, 235, 277, 225 and 237. It still makes me feel good to see those numbers lined up like that.

I slackened off some from there, but still led the tournament after 24 games. Then, for reasons I also still don't understand, I hit a wall. One day I was King Kong and the next I was Mickey Mouse. Over the 24 games of match play I hardly beat a soul (my record was 7-16-1), and wound up in 16th place. But my scoring record still stands as I write this, so it was a more-memorable occasion than a 16th-place finish ordinarily would be.

I would have to turn 50 years of age, and graduate to the seniors' class, before I would win another major title. That came in the 1984 PBA Seniors Championship in Canton, Ohio. It was my first year of eligibility for the event, and all the so-called experts assumed that since I was still active on the national tour, while most of the other seniors weren't, I would breeze to the championship. I knew my competition in the tourney would include the likes of Dick Weber, Harry Smith, Bob Kwolek, Jim Schroeder and Glenn Allison. I never had an easy time beating those guys when we were all in our prime, so I couldn't figure why my passing 50 would make it easier.

It turned out that the experts were right, for a change. It was about the easiest tournament I ever won. The first day I rolled a 299 game, and never looked back. I was the leader after each day's play, once by more than 500 pins, and averaged 221 over the 36 games of qualifying and match play.

In the final game I met Jim Schroeder, who had eliminated Weber in the semi-final. It had been quite a few years since I'd qualified for a tourney in first place. It meant that I had to take just one match to win it all, but that the guy

I'd be facing would have the advantage of having bowled at least one previous game over the lanes. I was more than a little nervous, and I guess it showed in my bowling. I needed a spare and a strike in the tenth frame to hold off Schroeder, 206-191.

To tell you how keyed up I was, I was sitting on the bench after it was over, kind of looking out into space, and Ginny had to poke me a couple of times to get my attention. "Hey, remember me?" she finally said. I was like a boxer in the ring, waiting for the next round to begin.

I've bowled a dozen seniors events since, and while I haven't won another one, I've been among the top half-dozen finishers in most of them. I'd love to see a full-scale senior circuit catch on in bowling the way it has in golf. A lot of people over 50 play our sport, and I'm sure they'd get a kick out of watching their contemporaries perform. I think that Earl Anthony turning 50 in 1988 will be a big asset to the PBA in selling sponsors on backing more seniors' events. Stefanich, Dave Soutar, Nelson Burton Jr., and Dave Davis also will be eligible soon.

The question I'm asked more often than any other is how I think bowlers of the different eras I've seen would do against one another. I can answer that one simply. Guys like Bomar, Day, Krumske, Wilman, Norris, Dick Weber and Carter would be winners today, and Anthony, Roth, Holman, Petey Weber, Cook, Aulby, Husted and Williams would have won in the old days.

It's more difficult to dominate bowling today because there are more good bowlers than there used to be. I think that puts Anthony's 42-win record between 1970 and 1984 a bit above the one Carter established when he won just about everything in sight between about 1955 and 1965. In terms of excellence over a longer period of time, I think Dick Weber takes the prize. Like me, he's won major championships in each of the last four decades. My aim is to stretch my wins over five decades starting in 1990. I'll be only 57 years old then—just a kid.

7

Staying in Shape

It should go without saying—but I'll say it anyway—that nobody lasts past age 50 in a highly competitive professional sport without staying in good physical condition. I've been fortunate that I've been blessed with good size and natural strength, and that those things were supplemented by an early life of hard work. I firmly believe that if our young people aren't as fit as they should be, the luxuries of modern life are mostly to blame. Our children today travel in $25,000 school buses to $250,000 school gyms to get a half-hour workout. When I was growing up, we walked to school and worked hard afterward, so we didn't need to work out.

Past a certain age, though—around 30 for most people—natural gifts tend to wane, and we must make a more conscious effort to exercise, eat right and get plenty of rest. Goodness knows, enough has been written about those subjects in the last few years to fill a library, much less a chapter in a book that's primarily about other matters. But I think that a few things need to be emphasized and reexamined, so I intend to have my say.

I know that a lot of you are wondering why it's important for a bowler to be fit. You've seen the pros bowl on television, and know that some of us aren't exactly Adonises. It's true that good bowlers come in various sizes and shapes, and that some of us weigh a bit more than we should. Furthermore, I can think of quite a few top pros over the years who weren't exactly models of temperate living. Bowling and beer seem to go together like liver and onions, and with beer companies sponsoring so many of the top teams in the 1940s and '50s, it wasn't uncommon to see the boys tilt a few samples of their sponsors' products after a hot evening on the lanes.

A couple of my old buddies, Billy Hardwick and Earl Johnson, had a particular fondness for the brew. They'd sometimes room together on the road, and could down as much as a case of beer between them *between blocks of games* during a tournament day. Billy liked to joke that those ''12-ounce curls'' were his weight training. I wasn't about to argue with his method; he made the ABC Hall of Fame, after all. Come to think of it, so did Earl.

A sadder story is that of Junie McMahon, who might have been the greatest bowler ever if a drinking problem didn't cut short his career and, eventually, his life. Junie was a big, sturdy guy whose delivery was the best combination of strength and smoothness I've ever seen. You could balance a glass of water on his head on his approach, and he'd never spill a drop. He was named Bowler of the Year in 1950 at age 38, and won the All-Star the next year, but an overfondness for liquor led him into decline after that. He suffered a stroke in 1959, and never bowled competitively again. He died in 1974.

Bowlers, though, aren't the only athletes who have run afoul of, or thrived despite, bad living habits. Those two great New York Yankees, Babe Ruth and Mickey Mantle, shared a famous ability to hit the long ball and an equally famous fondness for a tall, cool one or three after the game. Most of the best bowlers I've known over the years, though, have been both superior athletes and conscientious exercisers. Don Carter, for example, was a former minor-league baseball player whose strength was extraordinary; how else could he get so much power on his ball with that weird, "tip-toe" approach of his? He was a devotee of long-distance running long before that form was fashionable. Earl Anthony, the top bowler of the late 1970s and early 1980s, was another ex-baseball player who always kept himself in first-class shape.

Like most athletes, I've had my share of physical problems over the years. When I was about 30 years old, I had back aches that were traceable partly to the fact that one of my legs is a quarter-inch shorter than the other, and I had to search a long time before finding an orthopedic shoe insert that would make up for the difference while being flexible enough not to bother me when I bowled. The same examination that revealed the discrepancy in leg lengths also showed that one of my feet turned out slightly. I went to bed for about six months wearing a pair of boots joined by a steel bar that turned that foot inward. I gotta tell you, those boots didn't do much to improve my marital happiness! I dropped a ball on my big toe once, and bowled for weeks with a hole cut in my shoe. I've suffered from gout (but no more) and pulled muscles in various places.

Still, I've usually enjoyed excellent health and I've never been a slouch in the strength or flexibility departments. Well into my forties I could touch the heels of my hands to the ground without bending my knees (I can still get my knuckles down) and I could do fingertip pushups with the best of them. A few years ago I was bowling in Puerto Rico. There was a power failure in my hotel, so I walked down the 23 floors from my room to the lobby. Then I discovered that I had forgotten something upstairs, and made the trip back and forth to get it with scarcely a puff. I'll match myself against any 53-year-old guy in America for all-around fitness.

I'm often asked if I think bowling is good exercise. It certainly is if you roll 20 to 25 games a day, like I do. If you're talking about bowling once a week, three lines in a league, well, that's not much, maybe the equivalent of a brisk walk in the park. But don't sell it short. For older and sedentary people, it's an adequate day's workout, and because it involves different muscle groups (arms and shoulders to roll the ball, legs and back to support you while you're doing it) it's better exercise than many other things you could do. As a rule, though, being in good shape will do more for your bowling than bowling will do to get you in good shape. If you aspire to be a better-than-average bowler, and if you are of middle age or older, a regular program of physical conditioning is in order.

Flexibility

The foundation of any workout regimen should be a series of exercises designed to improve your flexibility. That's especially important for people of middle age or beyond, whose muscles don't have the spring of those of younger people. In this and other areas, *be careful not to try too much too soon.* That's the way you get hurt.

Start by putting both hands against a wall and one leg well behind the other. Stretch forward and downward on the back leg, allowing the front leg to bend deeply. Then change legs and stretch forward on the other one. This will loosen your calf muscles. Standing with both feet together and raising up on your toes a few times will have a similar effect. It won't hurt to do both those things.

I *don't* recommend that people bend straight down from the waist from a standing position to touch their toes. This can lead to back trouble. A better way to stretch your hamstring muscles—the big ones in back of your thighs—is to sit down with your legs extended in front of you and lean forward over one knee and then the other. Try to keep your legs straight when you do this, but if they bend a bit, it's no big deal. Do this exercise slowly, without bouncing up and down; that's the sort of sudden, pulling motion you should avoid. Work into this exercise gradually, trying to bend a little more each day.

While you're still sitting, put the bottoms of your feet together in front of you with your knees bent out. Holding your feet with both hands, bend forward slowly from the waist and try to touch your head to your feet. This will stretch your groin muscles.

You can begin upper-body stretches standing with your feet shoulder-distance apart and your hands on your hips. Lean to the left as far as you can, and then lean to the right. Do this a few times. Then reach back and try to touch the back of your left knee with your left hand followed by the back of the right knee with the right hand. This will complete your side stretches and, maybe, take something off those love handles that some guys have just above their hips.

Next, still standing, entwine your hands behind your head and twist your body one way and then the other, as far as it will go. Do this a dozen or so times. Then lock one hand in the other and pull sideways in turn. This will stretch the long muscles running down each side of your body.

Head and neck exercises come last with me, although I suppose you can do them in any part of your routine. All I do is turn my head a few times, slowly, as far as it will go in every direction—left, right, back and forward. Restricted neck movement is a problem with many people over 50, and regular stretching exercises will help you avoid it.

Cardio-Vascular Fitness

Every exercise program should include something that will get your heart pumping faster, which is the plain way of saying the fancy phrase above. There are a wide range of activities that will accomplish this. I've read that swimming is the best cardio-vascular exercise, and the best general one, for that matter, because it involves all the major muscle groups with none of the pounding of running. I used to swim in the summers when I was a kid, but my schedule doesn't permit it now. So many smart people recommend swimming, though, that I can only concur.

I don't run, and I don't recommend that other people do, especially on hard surfaces. I know that this is a controversial subject in fitness circles, and that I'm not qualified to contribute greatly to the debate. However, almost everyone I know who runs regularly has, or has had, some fairly serious back, knee, ankle, shin, or foot problems, and I've never wished any of those on myself. My common sense tells me that running on the streets or sidewalks can't be good for your bones and joints, and that if you run on the grass in the parks you stand a chance of stepping in a hole and twisting something.

The other three main choices for a heart-pumper are bicycling, getting a stationary exercise bike, or walking. I gotta go with either of the latter two, on grounds of safety. Bicycling is great exercise, but it usually involves tangling with cars and trucks that are a lot bigger than you are, and I want no part of that. An exercise bike gives you pretty much the same workout as real bicycling, and without the danger of bucking traffic. Moreover, you can fight boredom—the biggest enemy of repetitive exercise—by watching television while you pedal.

But the more I read and talk to people about exercise, the more convinced I am that regular walking is about the best thing a middle-aged person can do. An arm-swinging, hour-long walk three or four days a week, fast enough to raise a sweat, combines all of the requirements for cardio-vascular fitness with none of the physical drawbacks of running, the expense of buying an exercise bike, the dangers of city bicycling, or the inconveniences of getting to and from a swimming pool. You can walk anytime, anywhere, with anyone, wearing almost anything. The only equipment you really need is a comfortable pair of shoes.

I don't follow a regular walking routine because I figure I put in all the miles I need on the lanes. Still, I make it a point to walk instead of ride whenever I can, and unless I'm in the Empire State Building or other skyscraper, I'll rarely take an elevator going up or down stairs. When I walk, I make sure that my back is straight and chin is level. I had some back problems a few years ago which a specialist traced partly to lazy posture. Firming-up my walk helped make the back pains go away.

Another thing you can do for your back is to get a chair, put a pillow on its seat, and lay on the floor next to it with your legs bent and your lower legs resting on the pillow, for no more than 20 minutes. This takes the stress off your back and elevates your legs to improve blood circulation. I do that a couple of times a week for its relaxation value alone.

Muscle Toning

A couple of light exercises will improve your general muscle tone and set you up for a specific program geared to helping your bowling. For my money you can't beat the two old re- liables—pushups and situps—for this purpose.

I don't overdo the pushups because I'm afraid that too many of them will overdevelop the "lat" muscles under my armpits and interfere with my arm swing in bowling. Still, I do pushups several times a week, usually a half-dozen sets of 10 each. It's the sort of pushaway exercise that imitates the bowling motion and utilizes the muscles used in propelling the ball.

I also do situps regularly, raising my shoulders off the ground about a foot making sure to keep my knees well bent to ease the strain on my back. Abdominal fitness is an essential ingredient in any exercise program. If you're just starting to exercise, increase your situps gradually, starting with maybe 12 or 15 and working up to three sets of 20 each. The exercise is best done with nothing holding down your feet, but it's a good idea to work into that, too. Put your feet under a piece of furniture at first, making sure to cushion them with a pillow or rolled-up towel.

Getting Specific About Bowling

It's important to know that the physical requirements of various sports are different, and that once you have achieved an acceptable level of general fitness you should tailor your training to your sport's specific demands. For an extreme example of this, consider the Japanese Sumo wrestler. His huge belly, thighs and butt make him a comic figure in the United States, but, in fact, he's built perfectly for his sport, which requires him to lift and throw his opponent from a ring without being lifted and thrown himself. He doesn't look like much against a Mr. America-type, with the latter's bulging arm and chest muscles, but Mr. America wouldn't last 15 seconds against a Japanese "fat boy" in a Sumo ring.

Let's compare a couple of more familiar sports: football and basketball. Football mainly requires quick, almost explosive, bursts of energy against the resistance of opposing players. A football player must work hard to build the pushing muscles of his arms, shoulders, chest, thighs and buttocks. Basic specific football exercises involve lifting heavy weights with both arms (the press) or with both legs pushing together (squats). The basic unit of running in the sport is the 40-yard dash.

Basketball players are lean of build and must expend energy in fairly equal amounts over a long period of time. Long-distance running, usually provided by participation in the sport itself, is a must. Thigh and calf exercises must promote jumping ability, but not at the expense of developing those muscles to the point where running is inhibited. Upper-body weight training is limited to low-weight, high-repetition exercises designed to improve stamina.

In bowling, you must move along a path, slide, and roll a heavy ball towards a target 60 feet away. This requires arm strength in the fully extended position, back and lower-body flexibility and, most of all, good balance. It most certainly doesn't require the heavy, bunchy muscles you get from most of the weight-lifting exercises people do today, no matter how good they make you look on the beach.

Claims to the contrary notwithstanding, there is no ideal physique for a bowler. It used to be thought that short people were best suited to the sport because their low-to-the-ground stature gave them better ball-rolling mechanics, but the prominence on the PBA tour of such tall guys as six-feet-seven Steve Cook, six-feet-four Sam Flanagan, six-feet-three John Gant and me (I'm six-feet-two), belies that. What's important, I think, is good bodily proportions, including shoulders that are slightly wider than the hips to insure a smooth arm swing, and arms that are neither unusually long nor short.

A bowler needs smooth, elongated muscles and the stamina to repeat a difficult motion—the precise delivery of a 16-pound ball—again and again over a short period of time. He must be certain that any exercises he does will circumscribe *a full range of motion,* imitating those used in the approach and ball release.

The most useful devices I've found to help me accomplish this were shown to me by Bob Gajda, a noted physical therapy and fitness specialist in Chicago who has counseled many top athletes, and they couldn't be simpler. They include a thick, six-foot-long rubber line with a loop at each end, and some long, heavy rubber bands I can buy at any stationery store.

One beauty of both the rubber rope and the bands is that I can take them anywhere and use them anytime. The line fits easily into my suitcase. I can put the rubber bands in my brief case and exercise my hands and arms by pulling them while I'm sitting in an airplane or a car as a passenger.

I'll hook one end of the rubber line over a doorknob or other anchor and take the other loop in my hand. Then I'll go through my full ball-delivery motion against its resistance. I'll exercise my legs by swinging them, one at a time, on the line with one foot looped and the other end secured. Increasing the difficulty of the exercise involves only moving farther from my anchor, which increases the tension on the line. Doing these stretching exercises repetitively improves both my strength and flexibility.

Whenever I exercise one leg in this manner, I stand on the other leg without holding on to anything. This introduces the element of *balance,* without which good bowling is impossible. Under Bob Gajda's guidance, I've done quite a few things to try to improve my balance, such as walking on beams and walking with my eyes closed.

A gadget that Gajda introduced me to has been particularly helpful in improving my strength as well as balance. It's a balance board composed of a 12-inch by 16-inch piece of upholstered wood, three-quarters-inch thick, with a piece of two-by-four attached to its center and rounded at the end. An illustration is below. My neighbor, Roy Raffaelli, made one up for me in his basement workshop, and you might do the same.

I use the board in a number of ways. Standing on it frontwards, and holding on to a wall or piece of furniture, I lean on one leg and the other to loosen my hips. Then I let go of whatever I've steadied myself on and try to balance myself on the board alone. It takes some practice, but I've become pretty good at it.

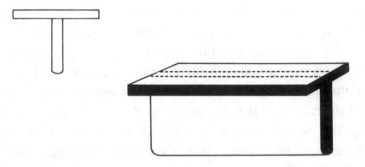

Standing on the board sideways, with the center-board under my feet, I rock back and forth to stretch my calf muscles. When I'm really feeling frisky, I put my hands on the sides of the board running frontwards and do pushups, trying to equalize my weight at the same time. A few pushups done that way are worth a couple dozen on a flat floor. I don't recommend this to you, though, until you're in very good shape. In general, of course, walking with good posture is the best thing anyone can do to improve his balance, and you needn't be an athlete to do that.

The other element I strive to include in my exercise routine, which is closely related to balance, is *body symmetry*. Maintaining symmetry is a particular problem for bowlers, because our sport tends to overdevelop the side of the body that delivers the ball. Tennis players have this problem, too. Rod Laver, the old Australian tennis star, was nicknamed "Popeye" because of his huge forearm on his left, or hitting, side. It's not just the action arm that gets too much work in sports, by the way. I've noticed that right-handers tend to lean to the right when they walk, and left-handers to the left, indicating that they favor that whole side.

I'm right-handed, so my right side gets most of the work when I bowl. I compensate for that by emphasizing my left arm and leg when I exercise. If I'm pulling on my rubber line, for instance, I'll do 15 pulls from the left and 10 from the right. I always try to carry things like suitcases and bowling bags lefty, and even make it a point to open doors and windows lefthanded. Every little bit helps.

Hands and feet also are important to bowlers, and I do things to develop mine. The best hand exercise I've come across was passed on to me many years ago by a boxer I met while working out at Stan Sarbaneck's gym in Chicago's Police Academy. Take a newspaper and spread it out flat on a table. Put your hand in the center of one sheet and start crumbling it with your fingers until you've reduced it to a small ball. Then change hands and do it to another sheet. Do several sheets with each hand. It's a great hand-strengthener, and involves no risk of injury.

A bowler's hands should be soft as well as strong because feel is important in the sport, and because cracks or cuts in the skin can be a real problem. I put creams on my hands just as my wife does, and I go her one better by rubbing in a good layer of Vaseline one night a week and going to bed wearing cotton worker's gloves (you can buy them in any hardware store for a few dollars). If I get a bruise or sore on a finger of my throwing hand, I'll cut a hole in a potato and stick it in there for awhile. It reduces the soreness and makes it heal faster.

Hand care should extend to the lanes. If a person's hands tend to be sweaty or oily, rubbing them with a slice of lemon or lemon juice a half-hour or so before bowling can help. Also, a slightly damp towel often can do a better job than a dry one of keeping oily hands prepared between shots.

The best thing a bowler can do for his feet is to wear good-fitting shoes all the time, and own a good pair of bowling shoes. No way you're going to bowl your best with rented shoes on your feet. The best foot exercise I've found consists of taking a Coca-Cola or other bottle with side ridges and, while seated, rolling it back and forth with the bottoms of my feet. That exercises small foot muscles and improves blood circulation. In addition, it feels good.

One final word on exercise. I do not, repeat, not, subscribe to the saying "No pain, no gain." Pain is your body's way of telling you that something is wrong, and when you feel it, you should stop whatever you are doing. If you have a history of illness, don't embark on any exercise program without your doctor's approval. If you're just beginning to exercise again after a layoff, ease into your program a little at a time. You're less likely to get hurt that way, and more likely to stick with it.

Taking Care of Your Insides

I firmly believe that what you put into your body is as important as what you do with the outside of it. I don't smoke and I don't drink hard liquor. The extent of my alcohol consumption is a beer on a hot afternoon. I never developed either the tobacco or alcohol habits, so I've never had to break myself of them. I guess that makes me fortunate.

I've also never hesitated to try to improve on nature when I thought it was worthwhile. I say that's because I'm a great believer in science and the perfectability of humankind.

Others have said it's because I'm a sucker for a story. Maybe both things are right.

Twelve or 15 years ago my hair began falling out in earnest. I tried everything to save it. Someone told me to rub peanut oil into my scalp, so I did. I used every sort of patent hair-restorer I could get my hands on. All had the same result, which was zero.

On one of my trips to Japan, I noticed that all the men there had thick, dark, terrific heads of hair. One fellow I asked said he thought it was because of the seaweed in their diets. I bought seaweed and ate it, but kept losing hair. Then I put seaweed on my head at night and covered it with a bathing cap. Not only didn't it keep my hair from falling out, but it also turned my scalp black, and Ginny threatened to divorce me over the smell.

I finally got hair transplants, which involved taking hair plugs from the back and sides of my head, where healthy hair grew, and putting them into the bald areas. A friend of mine, Dr. Kenneth Skaar of Rockford, Illinois, did the job. It hurt, but every time I look in the mirror I'm glad I did it. I think you're as young as you feel, and looking younger makes me feel that way.

I've read a lot about vitamins, and I've been taking them for many years. At one time I took 164 vitamin tablets a day, large doses of just about everything on the market except vitamins A and D, which accumulate in your system and can cause buildup problems if you overuse them. I took so many vitamins that I practically rattled when I walked. My philosophy was that by taking them all I'd get the ones I needed, and the rest would go through me. I've cut back to about a dozen vitamin capsules a day now, mostly C, E and

B-complex. I feel good, and rarely get colds, so I guess they're working.

I've put a lot weirder stuff than vitamins in my stomach. Somebody once told me about a nutritional supplement called "Tiger's Milk," and I used to scarf it mixed with milk and raw eggs. I remember whipping up one batch in a Las Vegas hotel room I shared with Don Carter. The mere look of it was enough to drive Don downstairs to the bar.

Another time I was touted on something called "dessicated liver," which was supposed to turn you into superman. It was an ugly brown powder that came in a can and smelled terrible. I would have thrown it away on the spot except that I'd told Don Russell, the bowler I was rooming with at the time, how wonderful it was for you. I put a couple of spoonsful into my blender with milk and chugged some down. It tasted so awful I felt like I was going to wretch, but Russell was there, so I smiled and kept right on drinking. I don't think I kept it down more than 10 seconds before making a bee-line for the bathroom.

I eat only *real* food now and take care not to overeat. I also eat only compatible foods. I got my ideas on that score some 20 years ago from Chuck Bernardi, a pharmacist from Highwood, Illinois, the Chicago suburb where Ginny grew up. It was his theory that certain foods digest easily together and other foods don't, and that you're best off only combining those that do in the same meals. I've noticed that this same theme has been popping up in diet books that have come on the market in recent years.

Bernardi believed that not mixing starches and proteins would increase your energy and minimize weight gain. He thought that you should eat high-protein foods like meat and eggs separately from starchy things like bread, potatoes and pasta. He didn't think that sugary foods, like most desserts, should be eaten less than two hours after lunch or dinner. If nothing else, waiting two hours before dessert means that you'll eat fairly few of them.

I'm not fanatical about my way of eating. If I'm on the road at lunch time, or in a hurry, I'll sometimes mix meat and bread in a sandwich, or if I'm bowling a tournament I'll sometimes eat desserts with dinner because I know I need the extra energy. But for the most part I separate food categories along the lines Bernardi suggested. For example, I'll have an omelet for breakfast one morning and toast and potatoes the next, but I'll rarely have them together. Similarly, I'll eat chicken, fish or steak with vegetables or a salad, but not with rice or potatoes, and if I have a pasta dish it'll be with tomato or other vegetable sauce on it, not meat or cheese.

I like chicken and fish better than red meat, and I understand that's a healthy preference. The same goes for my aversion to salt. Ginny and I don't keep salt around the house. There's natural salt in many foods, and most prepared foods, like canned soups, already have too much salt in them.

I eat three meals a day, with dinner usually finishing before 6 p.m. Except for a late dessert about once a week, or an occasional piece of fruit, I don't eat between the end of dinner and breakfast the next morning. I read where that's a good practice, too.

What and when I eat depends partly on when I'm going to bowl. I make it a rule never to go on the lanes with a full stomach. Carbohydrates—the starchy foods, mostly—give you quick energy, so if I'm bowling in the morning I'll try to eat a spaghetti dinner, and if I'm bowling in the afternoon I'll have a big breakfast of pancakes. I'll save most of the muscle-building protein meals for between tournaments, and make sure that my meal before I go on the lanes—usually at least two hours before—is a light one.

I suggest that you eat like I do on your bowling night. If your team goes on in the early evening, eat a pasta or pancake lunch and put off dinner until after you bowl. If you're to bowl at 8 p.m. or later, either eat a light snack around six o'clock or put off your high-carbohydrate lunch until 3 or 4 p.m.

My fellow pros and I don't drink beer while we're bowling (it's a rule), and I don't suggest that you do, either, if you're in a tournament or important match. But if you're in your regular league, or bowling just for fun, I don't see anything wrong in having a brew or two. Bowling is supposed to be recreational, and if a beer or highball helps you to relax, why not have one?

Wake Me at Noon

The last part of a good physical regimen is adequate sleep, and I've always been a champ at that. If I wasn't a sound sleeper, Joe Norris, the old joker, wouldn't have been able to artfully rearrange my hotel rooms on me when our Tri Par Radio team went on the road back in the Fifties.

The all-time champion sleeper among the professional bowlers was Georgie Howard, who won five tour tournaments before retiring about 10 years ago. He could fall asleep in front of a television set while a movie was on, wake up two hours later, and tell you everything that happened on the screen.

I can sleep in cars, trains or planes, sitting or standing, day or night. I once fell asleep on a bench during an evening tournament in Long Island, New York, after flying in from filming some television bowling shows in Chicago earlier the same day. Another time, while leading the Paramus Open in New Jersey in 1965, my hotel forgot my wake-up call, and I opened my eyes at 12:30 p.m., a half-hour before I was supposed to bowl on the final day. I dressed and covered the 15 miles between the hotel and bowling center in about 25 minutes, five minutes short of being eliminated for tardiness. I didn't wake up fully for an hour more, but I bowled well enough to stay in position to win the tournament with a late surge.

I'll occasionally have trouble sleeping, usually just before a tournament. I try not to let that bother me. I figure that my body will get the sleep it needs, and if I don't get it one night I'll make up for it the next. I'll often take a catnap the day after a rough night.

Before I go out and bowl during a tournament, I'll try to get away by myself somewhere and stretch out for 15 or 20 minutes. I try to relax my body completely, make my mind an absolute blank, and just give in to the universe. Negative thoughts are cast aside. I may doze or just sit there; it doesn't really matter. When I get up, I always feel calmer and stronger than I did when I laid down.

What Goes First

I'm the oldest regular on the PBA tour, and people always ask me how I've been able to last so long. As I've outlined here, physical conditioning certainly plays a role. But there's more to it than that. It's my observation that the old saying "the legs go first" doesn't apply to bowling, or, probably, golf and other sports that don't require quickness afoot. I think what goes first is the athlete's *desire to excel,* which expresses itself in his willingness to learn his game from the ground up and put in the work needed to adapt his style to the internal and external changes that are a part of every field of endeavor.

Most athletes go as far as their natural skills take them, and no farther. That's why professional careers in physically demanding sports like football, basketball, hockey, boxing and baseball average just four or five years, and why golfers, bowlers and tennis players rarely stick around for more than 10 years. Their legs don't go; research shows that people can sustain peak physical performance well into their 30s. I think it's that they let down mentally, giving their competition the chance to pass them.

Higher salaries and prize money in professional sports have been a powerful force in motivating athletes to do what it takes to stay competitive. In baseball, you've got a flock of guys over 40 still going strong, like Phil and Joe Niekro, Tommy John, Nolan Ryan, Don Sutton and Reggie Jackson. Pete Rose broke Ty Cobb's career-hits record when he was 44. Sam Snead won tournaments on the pro golf tour after 50. Jack Nicklaus won the Masters in 1986 at age 46. Willie Shoemaker rode the Kentucky Derby winner that same year at 54!

Sure, those guys stay fit, but they have the brains to stay sharp, too, and, by me, that's the essential ingredient. I'm honored to be counted among them.

8

Better Bowling: Getting the Right Equipment

Having proper equipment is essential for success in any sport, but some bowlers give it less attention than it deserves. I guess this stems in part from the fact that it's not necessary to own your own ball or shoes to bowl, because you can rent them, cheaply, at your local bowling center. I suppose, too, that to the uninitiated most bowling balls look alike (round and black), and the assumption is that they also perform alike.

As I mentioned in chapter 6, there have been great advances in bowling-equipment technology over the past 15 or so years, and we pros are well aware of them. Using the right ball is important, of course, but I think that some pros may overestimate how much a particular ball can affect their scores. But that's a natural reaction to the tough competitive situation they're in. Relatively speaking, a novice or intermediate-level bowler can show far more improvement by acquiring the right ball, shoes and accessories than can a pro, and far more quickly. Owning the right gear also is a necessary first step in any program to improve the mechanical aspects of your game. No one with any desire to bowl even moderately well should take to the lanes with rented balls or shoes.

Some people start off wrong in buying bowling equipment by looking for bargains rather than going to a place that can offer advice and service. I'm talking about your local bowling pro shop. The men and women behind the counters in those stores are really kinds of bowling doctors, who can listen to and investigate your symptoms, and prescribe "cures." Buying balls and shoes should involve an *exchange of information* with them about your game and the conditions under which you bowl. Also, you should realize that buying a bowling ball is rarely a one-stop proposition. A ball that feels good in the store doesn't always feel good in action, and alterations often are required. A good shop person can look at your hands after you bowl, see where your ball is rubbing, and make the proper adjustments. He may charge a bit more than the discount store down the street, but it's likely he'll give you more than your money's worth in service over the long run.

Buying a ball requires decisions in three basic areas: **weight, grip,** and **ball reaction.** Your pro-shop proprietor can assist you in these, but the basic choices will be yours. Thus, you'll need to take an honest inventory of your game and physique before proceeding.

Ball Weight

You might think that getting a correctly weighted ball is the easiest part of your purchase decision, but it's my observation that it's the thing most recreational bowlers get wrong. Many of them, especially the men, use balls that are too heavy. This throws off their deliveries, breeds injuries and bad habits, and makes later corrections all but impossible.

Bowling balls range in weight from six to 16 pounds. The lighter balls are for junior bowlers, aged six to 11 or 12, and small women. A woman weighing 110 pounds or less, and who bowls no more than once a week, shouldn't use more than a 12-pound ball.

From there, things get more complicated, depending not only on bodily size and strength, but on physical coordination and bowling expertise. A physically fit woman who is well coordinated and bowls frequently can be quite capable of handling a 16-pound ball; my wife, Ginny, who has never weighed more than 115 pounds, used one with ease while she was winning local and state amateur championships years ago. On the other hand, the 200-pound man who has a paunch, works in an office, and bowls once a week would be better off using a 15-pounder, or even a 14.

The problem with a lot of men, of course, is that they think it isn't *macho* to use less than the heaviest ball. But I'd estimate that 90 percent of the people who bowl, men included, should *not* use a 16-pounder. A number of top players, including Marshall Holman, Mike Aulby and Jim St. John, have won tournaments with 15-pound balls, and more of the younger pros are experimenting with balls of that weight, reasoning that the increased rotation they can put on the lighter ball will more than compensate for the loss of weight-caused impact. I endorse that line for non-pros, too.

I've always used the 16-pound ball, but I realize that one of these days, when I start feeling my age, I'm going to have to move to a lighter one. Too many older bowlers persist in using the 16-pounder past the point where they can control it adequately. Younger players should move *up* in ball weight as their strength and skill grows, but I do not recommend a 16-pounder to anyone, of any age, who bowls less than twice a week.

Ball Grips

There are three basic ball grips: **conventional, semi-fingertip,** and **fingertip.** Choosing among them should depend on your hand strength, style, and skill. Generally speaking, novice and intermediate bowlers, women, and young bowlers just starting out are best advised to use the conventional grip, which is drilled to permit the third and fourth fingers to enter the ball at the second knuckle. The conventional grip maximizes ball control and is best suited to any bowler whose normal shot is more or less straight. I'd say that about 85 percent of all bowlers use it, most of them for their entire life in the sport.

The statistical picture is almost the opposite among the male bowling pros, about 95 percent of whom use either the fingertip or semi-fingertip grip, in which the fingers enter the ball at the first knuckle. It takes a strong hand to control the ball with that alignment, and makes shooting spares harder. The latter difficulty usually is more than compensated for by the increased rotation, or hook, that can be generated by a fingertip-controlled ball, which translates into more impact in the pocket, and more strikes.

Just about everyone starts bowling using the conventional grip and, like I've said, most people stick with it. But almost all bowlers who desire to join the game's upper echelons graduate to a fingertip grip somewhere along the line. There are different schools of thought about when and how this transition should occur. I think a bowler ought to have a sound basic delivery, stronger-than-normal hands, and average at least 170 before moving to the semi-fingertip grip, which doesn't extend the fingers quite as far as a full-fingertip. I think he or she should be averaging 190 or better before moving to the full-fingertip.

Dedicated young bowlers can make this journey quickly. Most male professionals mastered the full-fingertip grip while still in their teens, like I did. For less-active bowlers, it may take several years to even try the semi-fingertip, and the switch may involve a temporary reduction in average because of the greater difficulty in picking up spares. No bowler with high aspirations, though, should refuse to try the fingertip grips on grounds of difficulty, because it is well-nigh impossible to average better than 200 without a ball that has considerable hooking action.

The one warning that I have about moving to an extended-finger grip is directed at men and women of middle age or beyond. Too many solid older bowlers—people averaging between 170 and 185—make a belated switch to a fingertip grip in hopes of emulating the pros and adding a few pins to their scores. What they often get instead are hand and wrist injuries, and they risk throwing away their spare games to boot. They could get their higher scores easier by practicing harder on making their spares, and with less physical wear and tear. It's no disgrace to recognize that you'll never be a pro, or even a local ace. In fact, if you've reached middle age and haven't made it yet, you probably already suspect that you won't, and that less lofty goals are appropriate.

Ball Hardness

The business of finding a ball to fit your style and the lane conditions where you usually bowl involves choosing among a wide and growing variety of balls on the market. The most easily identifiable of their characteristics pertain to their cover sheens and hardness. There are shiny balls and dull ones, "hard" ones and "soft" ones.

Time was when you could tell just about all you needed to know about a ball by looking at it. Balls that were shiny also were "hard," and best suited straight-ball bowlers who bowled on dry lanes. Balls that were dull-colored also had "soft" covers that would grip the lanes better than harder ones, and suited hook-ball bowlers. Things are more complicated now; you can find dull balls that have hard covers, and shiny ones that are soft. Still, the main guidelines usually still apply, and your pro-shop proprietor can assist you through the maze.

You'll have to help, though, because he can't tell by looking at you across the counter how you bowl, or where. You'll know, of course, whether you throw a straight ball or a hook, but speed also is part of the equation, and it's often overlooked. *If you throw a slow shot, chances are that you should buy a ball on the hard-shiny side of the spectrum, because its low-friction qualities will allow the ball to maintain energy once it comes out of its slide. If you throw a hard, fast shot, you probably should look among the soft, i.e., high-friction, balls to give it the lane-grabbing quality that will start it rolling in time to make it effective in the pocket.*

Most bowling centers keep approximately the same lane conditions throughout the bowling season. If you are unsure about them, ask the center's proprietor or an experienced bowler who frequents the place. Even so, you should be alert to the specific conditions that exist *when* you bowl. For instance, if the center oils its lanes in the afternoon, and you bowl in the first evening league, the likelihood is that you'll have oily conditions, and an oily-lane ball, usually a soft one, is in order. But if you bowl the second or third shift, the oil will have partially evaporated and been dispersed down the lanes by the previous bowlers, so you'll probably be better off with a ball that's a bit on the harder side.

If you bowl regularly at more than one center, or have tournament aspirations, it's a good idea to own, and always carry, two or more balls with differing degrees of friction. Don't make them so different, though, that you have to alter your normal style of delivery to be effective with them.

Ball Fit

The main service that your bowling pro shop will provide is a ball that fits right. Not everyone is equally adept at the art of measuring people for balls and drilling the holes at the proper places and angles, so it will pay you to ask around among bowlers you know, particularly the better ones, to learn where they have received satisfaction.

You won't be running the drill yourself, but there are a couple of terms related to ball fit that you should know. One is the **span,** which is the distance between the thumb hole and the finger holes, centered on the second knuckle in the conventional grip, and the first knuckle in the finger-tip grip. The other is the **bridge,** which is the distance between the two finger holes. The standard bridge is 3/8-inch, but it can be varied a bit to accommodate different hand sizes and releases. Generally speaking, hookers prefer a slightly wider bridge than people who throw a straight ball, particularly with a fingertip grip.

The main factor in a correct ball fit is the thumb hole, and the person who drills your ball will need a lot of feedback from you on this. Most people need a thumb hole that's snug enough to allow you to grip the ball firmly, but not so snug that it prevents a quick release. It's important to understand here that your hands aren't always the same size. They will swell on warm, humid days, and shrink on cold, dry ones. Some women's hands also swell during their menstrual periods. For most people, hand-swelling affects thumb size more than finger size. If you have a history of swollen hands, you should buy a ball that's a bit looser in the thumb than normal so that you won't have to widen the hole on days when your hands are swollen. You can carry inserts or tapes that will make the hole smaller when you need it. More about that later.

Ball Weight Distribution

Bowling balls may look perfectly balanced, but they are not. Material lost in the drilling of the thumb and finger holes must be compensated for by the addition of extra-heavy material in the area of the drilling. This is called the weight block, which usually is pancake shaped and thicker in the middle than at the edges. Here is a cross-section drawing of a typical bowling ball illustrating what one looks like.

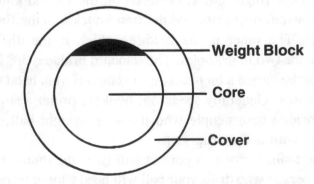

It is possible to affect the ball's action by the placement of the thumb and finger holes relative to the weight block. Again, placing those holes correctly is the job of the pro-shop driller, but he will need information from you to guide him. Following are some terms you should know when discussing ball-weight distribution.

A **zero-weighted** ball is drilled dead-center over the weight block, and, thus, has no weight bias. I recommend this to beginning bowlers who haven't yet established a style, and to persons who throw a more-or-less straight ball.

A **positive-weighted** ball is drilled just to the left of the weight block's center. It will hook slightly more than a zero-weighted ball in a right-hander's delivery, and the hook will come later. Most hookers prefer a slightly positive weighted ball because it gives their shots a slightly later hook, a phenomenon bowlers call "finish."

A **negative-weighted** ball is drilled just to the right of the weight block's center. Negative weighting will retard the size of the hook and cause it to occur sooner. People whose shots have too much hook sometimes have their balls drilled this way, although that condition is rare.

A **finger-weighted** ball is drilled with the finger holes closer to the center of the weight block than the thumb hole. It will hook later and more sharply than an oppositely drilled **thumb-weighted** ball, whose hook tends to be more gradual. Generally speaking, people looking for more ball "action" opt for finger weighting, while people more interested in control will choose thumb weighting.

Finally, most balls are drilled with a bit of **top weight,** a condition that occurs when the amount of material removed for the thumb and finger holes doesn't quite equal the weight of the weight block. The top weight of the ball before drilling usually is stated on the cover of the box a ball comes in. The label will say, for instance, 16 pounds, with two or three ounces of top weight. The difference between the amount of material removed in drilling (usually about three ounces for a conventional grip, or 2-1/2 ounces for a fingertip grip) and the original top-weight figure gives the final top weighting.

Top weighting makes a ball hook sharper and later than a no-top-weight ball, and most bowlers like this. Most of the better players use a ball that has a bit of top weight and a bit of positive weight. As important as those weighting schemes are, though, you still must release the ball correctly to make it behave as you wish. There is no magical-weighting formula for success.

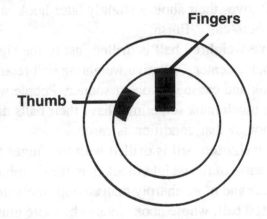

All of the ball-action patterns just described can also be obtained with the balls Ebonite is making with my double-weight block design, pictured above in cross-section. The differences will come in greater ball balance and stability. Double-weight-block balls will have a smoother trajectory than single-weight-block ones in both the straight and hooking modes.

Buying Shoes

Next to your ball, your bowling shoes are your most important pieces of equipment, and, in fact, an argument can be made that you should buy your own shoes first. You usually can find a house ball in the center where you bowl that will fit you decently, but rental shoes almost always come with slippery, leather soles for both feet because most proprietors don't want to bear the expense of stocking separate shoes for right- and left-handers. And it's easy to pick up bad delivery habits from bowling with improper footing.

The bowling shoes that people buy for themselves have a leather or elk-skin sole on the "slide" foot and a rubber sole on the other. This permits the bowler to combine slide and traction into a correct delivery. You will need bowling shoes with good ankle support, and the same snug fit you require from your street shoes. When you go to try yours on, wear the kind of cotton athletic socks you will wear when you bowl.

Other choices that come with buying bowling shoes have to do with getting perforated soles on the slide shoe, and different heel heights. Perforated soles have the effect of slowing your slide. I wear them at times, but that's strictly a matter of individual preference.

The same goes for the heel height. The standard bowling shoe heel measures 5/8-inch, the same as street shoes. But some bowlers, such as Jim Stefanich and Dick Weber, use a quarter-inch heel insert to raise them and shift their weight slightly forward. On the other side are the no-heel bowling shoes, similar to tennis shoes, that are increasingly coming on the market. Again, whether you wear them depends on how you feel most comfortable.

One thing I strongly recommend is that you wear in your bowling shoes any orthopedic supports that you normally wear in your street shoes. Failure to do this not only can throw off your game, but can also worsen your foot or back problem.

Gloves and Accessories

Every bowling store these days carries a wide variety of hand and wrist supports. They range from large, rigid devices that bristle with straps and extend halfway up the arm, to the simple, padded gloves that will keep your ball from resting on your palm during your delivery. The hand and wrist supports increase stability, thus aiding the repeatability of your delivery. I think more people should use them than actually do, expecially women and occasional bowlers. You'll probably save some money if you try out the ones your friends are using before choosing one of your own.

What to Wear on the Lanes

Anything that feels comfortable will do, but I think the best garments are a non-binding shirt and slacks for men, and a blouse and slacks or a medium-loose (but not too long) skirt for women. I notice a lot of league bowlers of both sexes wearing jeans and tee-shirts these days. I frown on that because tee-shirts can be too tight in the shoulders and upper arms, and the jeans material is too heavy for easy movement. The PBA dress code precludes us pros from wearing tee-shirts or jeans in tournaments on grounds of appearance, but few of us would wear them if we could.

(Our dress code also specifies that we wear socks on the lanes. Under-shorts are optional, but they have been strongly recommended since Mark Baker was revealed to be without them when he ripped his pants during a 1984 tournament in Miami. That quickly came to be known as the ''moon over Miami'' incident.)

The Bowler's Kit

No one should take to the lanes without a ''granny's bag'' of assorted items needed to cope with emergencies. Few of the contents will be used every day, but everything will be used sometime. I'm convinced that the surest way to cause any kind of bowling accident is to forget to bring the gadget you need to deal with it.

A bowler's kit should always include a towel to wipe your hands between shots and a couple of other hand-care items. These include a rosin bag for damp days, and a small jar of ''grip cream'' that makes the fingers a bit tacky on days in which the humidity is very low. People with oily hands might want to also pack a lemon that they can squeeze and rub into their hands before they bowl. Everyone should pack a nail clipper and file.

A bowler must be prepared to treat blisters. One application is a thin, gauze-like tape that comes with a liquid that resembles clear nail polish to hold it in place. The liquid dries in a minute or so, and gives the blister first-aid protection until it can be treated later. I usually use a different product called ''Flexi-Patch,'' a thin, flexible tape similar to a Band-Aid that is applied directly to the blister and molds itself to the contour of the finger, hand or foot. I carry a small, sharp scissors to shape the patches, and often find it useful for other jobs as well.

If the skin covering a blister is broken, the wound must be disinfected and dressed immediately. If you can't do this and continue bowling, then stop bowling. Because of the threat of infection, a blister should be regarded as a serious medical problem. If you get them repeatedly on the same part of your bowling hand, chances are that the finger or thumb holes of your ball should be altered.

To adjust my bowling-ball holes on days when high humidity causes my hands to swell, I use a three-edged knife or a rattailed file as bevelers and a piece of fine sandpaper to smooth out rough edges and surfaces. Because I sometimes want to build up or change the pitch of a hole rather than widen it, I carry a tube of plastic wood. I pat a little where I want it to go, allow it to dry (this takes about 30 minutes if it is spread thinly), and smooth it with sandpaper. As far as I know, I was the first bowler to use plastic wood to adjust the grip of a bowling ball.

You might want to consider adjustable grips, which come with a key with which you can tighten or loosen the holes as needed. Other grip inserts are molded to duplicate the shape of your fingers and thumb. A lot of bowlers use them all the time.

Let's see what else is in my kit. A bottle of aspirin, some pencils and a small pad of paper to make notes about lane conditions, a candy bar for quick energy, a quarter in case I have to make a telephone call, and a hair comb. Hey, you never know when you might be interviewed on television!

Better Bowling:
Mechanics

I've taught bowling for many years in many different places, but one thing that never changes is the initial reaction of most of the people I have tried to help. After listening to my comments on their games, and trying to put one or two of my suggestions into practice, they'll shrug their shoulders apologetically and say they're sorry, but the changes don't "feel comfortable." Their assumption is that anything that doesn't immediately feel right for them can't possibly work.

I can understand that because of my experience with Hank Lahr, but that doesn't make my role as a teacher any easier. I could point out to my pupils that they have sought me out—and paid me (I'm a pro, after all)—to help them improve their scores, not make them feel better about doing what they've always done, and that a little temporary discomfort is a small additional price to pay for improvement. In truth, though, that's not satisfactory to them or me. What they are really saying is that I have confused them by asking them to think and bowl at the same time. It isn't the small physical adjustments I suggest that throw them off, but the necessity to connect their minds to what their bodies are doing, and they've never, or rarely, been asked to do that before.

This mind-body problem is more pronounced in bowling than in most other sports. The tradition of individual instruction that is so strong in golf and tennis has never caught on in bowling. One reason for this is that we bowling professionals have never organized ourselves around teaching the way that those in golf and tennis have. Another is that bowling *looks* like about the easiest thing in the world to do. You just pick up a ball and roll it towards the pins, right? Any child can do it.

Bowling isn't nearly as simple as it looks, though, for three main reasons. The first is the weight of the ball, which changes an easy, natural motion—the underhand swing—into something complex and difficult. The second is the deceptively small target area for the strike ball; a difference of no more than an inch at 60 feet can change a strike into a hard-to-pick-up split. Third and last are the lane-condition obstacles that the ball encounters on its way to the pins. The fact that these are not always readily apparent, the way trees, ponds, and sand traps are on a golf course, make them tougher, not easier to cope with.

Your average, self-taught bowler wakes up to the difficulties of the sport when he hits a scoring plateau, usually around 150, several years after taking it up. He'll ask his bowling buddies for advice, or read a book like this one in hopes of picking up a few tips. But by the time he has decided to try in earnest to raise his average, his habits—many of them bad—have become ingrained, and he has developed very definite notions about how his shots should "feel." Both his bad physical habits and rigid thinking bar his path toward improvement.

So my first—and, maybe, most important—piece of advice has nothing to do with how to roll a bowling ball. It's that you open your mind to new knowledge about the game and resolve to try to put to use what you learn, even though it might make you uncomfortable for a time. I think you'll be surprised at how quickly bowling better will make you feel better.

The next thing we have to talk about is style. This is a book (a chapter, really) and not a private lesson, so I can't diagnose anyone's particular problems or suggest specific remedies. Moreover, I'm well aware that instructional books turn off a lot of people by advocating a "classic" style that few novices or, even, professionals, can duplicate. When you turn on the television set and watch the many different ways that the current pros deliver the ball, or remember Don Carter winning all those tournaments with his weird, tip-toe approach and piston-motion arm swing, you well might wonder why anyone should bother to develop the so-called classic stroke.

The answer is that the classic style contains reference points that everyone can use to evaluate his own form, even if his total game couldn't pass for Ned Day's. If your footwork is off, compare it with the footwork of a classic-style bowler. Same with your arm swing and ball release. If adjustments are called for, they should be made *in the direction* of the classic style, if not duplicating it exactly. Youngsters and other people just starting out in bowling should model their games on the classic style as closely as possible. Not only is it tried and true, but its use also makes it easier to spot and remedy the flaws that crop up in everyone's delivery from time to time.

However, I do not recommend that people who have bowled for a number of years, and experienced some success, scrap their natural styles for the classic one. I think that rather, after an honest examination of your delivery, you should *identify and build off of your strong points*. If you have bowled for a number of years, and achieved even mediocrity, chances are that there is something good about your game. Using that as your foundation for improvement will provide the familiar ground that will make changes easier to incorporate, and knowing that you're doing something right should improve your general mental state.

Set Up and Approach

Before you take a step with a bowling ball in your hand, there are things you should know and do. I think that a lot of people's bowling problems stem directly from improper set-up procedures. And that's good, because they are the easiest to correct.

The first thing you should do when you get on the lanes is to **find your point of origin.** This will be the distance from the foul line where you will begin your approach on every ball you deliver. For a four-step approach, which I advocate, place your heels three or four inches in front of the foul line. Take four good-sized walking steps, plus a half step to allow for a slide. Then turn to face the pins and note where you are standing relative to the markings on the approach. You will then be properly placed to deliver the ball with an adequate slide and still finish well behind the foul line. I think it bears repeating that you should use the same mark for every ball you throw, strike or spare. Repeatability is an important key to better bowling, and you can't hope to achieve it if you begin every approach from a different spot.

There are basically three types of approaches—the three-step, four-step and five-step. Three-steppers usually are very large and strong men who feel that they have the muscle to propel their shots sufficiently with very little approach. They, and their style, are rare. The five-stepper is more widely used by smaller people for a longer approach that gives them more momentum. However, the first step in the five-step approach is usually really only a half step, a sort of motion-starter comparable to the "waggle" with which golfers start their swings. I used the first step of a five-step approach in that manner before Hank Lahr convinced me it was a complication I was better off without.

The most common and, I believe, best approach is the four-stepper which, for a right hander, goes right foot, left foot, right foot and slide that culminates in the release of the ball. Each step in the approach corresponds to a movement of the arm with the ball. The ball is pushed forward—away from the body—on the first step. On the second step, the ball is at arm's length, hanging straight down. On the third step, you should reach the height of your backswing. On the fourth, your front foot is sliding and the ball is coming through towards the pins like an airplane coming in for a landing. Let's go through that again:

Out on one.

Down on two.

Back on three.

Slide and roll on four.

The drawings below illustrate the correct body position on each of the four steps.

(1)   (2)   (3)   (4)

Now you are ready to bowl. Go to the ball return and pick up your ball. Place both hands on the outside of the ball, away from oncoming balls. That way, you won't risk getting your fingers smashed. Don't laugh. I've seen it happen plenty of times.

When you have your ball, hold it in both hands, or in your non-bowling hand only, until you are ready to assume your stance and take your approach to the foul line. This will keep your bowling hand relaxed and free of the ball's weight until it's time to bowl.

Where you stand in relation to the pins will depend on whether you throw a hook or a straight ball. If you are like most bowlers, and have a fairly straight shot (no one can throw a perfectly straight ball—your hand won't permit it), I recommend that you align your right shoulder with the *second arrow from the right,* in the pyramid of arrows imprinted on the lane 10 feet from the foul line. (Left-handers should align their left shoulder with the second arrow from the left.) Then point your feet *towards your target, not square to the lane.* In the case of a strike ball, you should face the

1-3 pocket. For a spare, face the pin for which you are shooting. The drawing below illustrates this very important point.

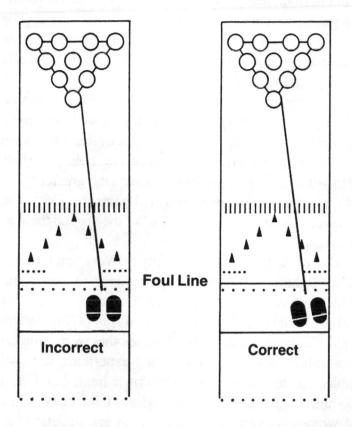

Your stance should be relaxed, with your feet slightly apart and your left foot (right foot for left-handers) a few inches in front of your right foot. Bend your knees and arch your back slightly. You'll know when your feet are properly placed when you can rock back and forth comfortably without being put off balance by the weight of the ball.

Your next consideration should be where you hold your ball in relation to your body. You don't want to hold it too far out in front, because that will throw your weight forward, onto your toes, and create the tendency to rush your approach and your shot. This is a common bowling mistake. I recommend that you hold it about waist high and with your elbow tucked into your side.

How high you hold your ball will determine the size of the pendulum arc, which, in turn, determines the height of your backswing and the speed of your delivery. The principle of the pendulum applies. The higher you hold your ball to begin with, the higher your backswing, the greater the arc, and the more natural speed you will generate. Conversely, the lower you hold the ball, the smaller the arc and the slower the speed.

One of the major changes in my delivery that Hank Lahr instituted during my long dry spell was to move the initial position of my ball from my waist to straight down, just in front of my right leg. The idea was that simplifying my stroke would eliminate some of the variables that were hampering repeatability. My strength and long experience in bowling enables me to handle a straight-down hold, but I do not recommend it to the occasional bowler. I think that most men, and women above average in strength and athletic ability, should hold their bowling balls about waist high in their stances. Smaller people, and those who need more speed on their delivery, should adopt a chest-high hold. Also, *the ball at starting point should be held towards your bowling side rather than in the center of your body.* This will help your arm clear your hips so the ball will swing on a straight line.

What's essential is that once you have found a hold that is comfortable and suitable to your form, you stick with it, shot after shot. We are again talking about *repeatability,* the cornerstone of a solid game. The drawings below illustrate a bowler at the "ready" position, her feet apart, knees slightly bent, and ball waist high and held on her throwing side.

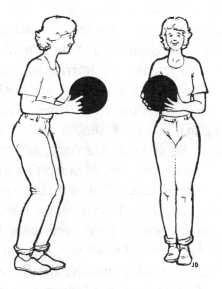

Bowling is a game of leverage, which in turn is a function of balance. If you are off balance in any direction—forward or backwards, left or right—your game surely will suffer. A good approach is one that maintains bodily balance at every stage.

The walk in your approach—and it's a *walk,* not a trot or a run—should be heel-and-toe, just like your gait on the street. Not only will concentration on getting your heels down first help prevent you from running, but the full-foot-down walk will provide the maximum of the balance and leverage we talked about before. It is well-nigh impossible to get any power on your ball, or hook it strongly, when you are lunging forward, your weight on your toes.

I don't suppose the advice to slow down is anything new. It's the first thing every bowling teacher tells every novice bowler, and, for the most part, it's appropriate. Probably the largest single mistake most bowlers make is to head for the line too fast. A rushed shot typically is a botched shot, lacking everything that's needed for success: balance, rhythm, power and alignment. Taking a small and slow first step is a good way to avoid a hurried approach.

I don't, however, wish to leave the impression that I think everyone should bowl at the same tempo. That would be as silly as saying that everyone should walk, eat, or think at the same speed. Some of us are fiery, action types whose natural pace is faster than that of others, so when we bowl, we should bowl a bit faster. I'm in that category, and so is Arnold Palmer, the golfer. Toscanini, the great musical conductor, had his orchestras play everything fast, so if he bowled, he probably would bowl fast, too. On the other side are the likes of my bowling buddy, Jim Stefanich, or Jack Nicklaus in golf. With them, the footwork goes "plop, plop, plop," regular and steady as a junkman's horse. You have to know yourself, and what works best for you.

Armswing

For my money, the armswing is the most important element in the bowling delivery. Look around the PBA tour and you'll see all sorts of footwork, some good and some not-so. But what you'll almost always see are great armswings. It is the arm, propelling the ball, and the fingers, turning it, which knock over the pins.

A good armswing begins in the "ready" position. Your bowling hand and forearm should be facing up, towards the ceiling. You should grip the ball firmly, but not so hard that your forearm or bicep tightens up. The next thing you must do is start your swing *in line with your shoulder* so your arm will clear your hip and swing straight back. Holding the ball towards your bowling-arm side during your set-up will facilitate this. People whose hips are wider than their shoulders will have difficulty managing a straight backswing. They should take care to keep their elbows as close to their sides as possible, avoiding the elbow "flare" that will rob them of power. Practicing with this point in mind will help you locate the best position of your arm and elbow during the swing. Once you've found it, keep it there.

We'll get to the mechanics of the hook later, but I think it's important to say here that your arm should *remain straight throughout your swing, whether you are throwing a straight ball or a hook,* and that any rotation you impart to the ball should come from your fingers. A common mistake novice bowlers make is to line up parallel to the foul line instead of to their target, and compensating by canting their arm-swings. A vital element in good bowling is to *align both your body and arm towards your target.* Let the pendulum be your guide.

The next point is the **release.** This is where everything you have done before comes together, for better or worse, to produce your shot. As you release the ball, your front knee should be bent, your back leg extended, your arm straight down your side and your trunk leaned slightly forward. Figure four on page 176 illustrates this.

The key to the release itself is *getting your thumb free of the ball smoothly.* If the thumb hole is too tight and you do not come out fast enough, your shot will veer to the left (for a right hander), in the same way that a golf shot is pulled. If your thumb comes out smoothly and you apply rotation with your fingers, the ball will touch the lane about a foot over the foul line, like the image I suggested before, of a plane coming in for a landing. On the other hand, if your thumb hole is too loose, you will drop the ball behind the foul line and you will not be able to apply finger rotation.

I think the **follow-through** is the most overrated part of the bowling delivery. If you do everything right through the point where you release the ball, there is no way that your follow-through will be anything but perfect. Conversely, if your armswing or release are poor, posing with your arm pointed gracefully at the ceiling won't do a bit of good. The follow-through is important, though, as a *mental extension of your shot.* You can use it as a reference point to see if your swing was on target. Then follow the ball with your eyes through the pins and into the pit.

The Head and Eyes

The position of the head and eyes during the shot deserves a separate heading, because I think it is widely misunderstood. You hear the phrase "keep your head down" in bowling almost as often as you do in golf, but in bowling it can be misleading because too many people interpret it to mean that they should put their chins on their chests and keep their eyes on the floor while they bowl.

I think it's far more useful to tell people to *keep their heads as steady as possible, and their eyes on their target* during their delivery. The target I use is not the pins or the pyramid of arrows about 10 feet down the lane, but the dovetails, or "piano keys," 15-18 feet out, where the maple boards that make up the front part of the lane meet the softer pine boards that make up the remainder. The picture below illustrates the place I mean.

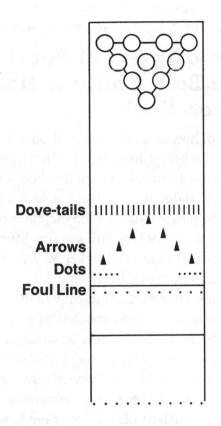

Sighting on the dove-tails rather than the arrows has two advantages. One is that the arrows are set at different distances from the foul line, so that using different arrows as a guide for your strike and spare balls, as you'll often do, will mean that you must alter your viewing distance from shot to shot, and this will impair repeatability. The dove-tails, on the other hand, are all in a line. Second, sighting along individual boards, rather than the more-widely-spaced arrows, will make it easier for you to make small adjustments in your shots. Later, in the chapter on bowling strategy, I will talk about how to use the dove-tails relative to the arrows.

The Three Types of Shots: Straight Ball, Shallow Hook and Large Hook

The question of how to hook the ball should be preceded by the question of whether to hook. Essentially, it's a choice between power and control. A shot that hooks is more powerful than one that doesn't because it attains a steeper angle of entry into the pins and its rotation increases pin "action." The negative is that a hooking ball is more difficult to control than a straight ball, and the hooker will more often miss spares than the straight-ball bowler.

I don't think anyone should attempt to throw a hook until he or she has learned the fundamentals of bowling, averages at least 160, bowls twice or more a week, and does some practicing. It's a tough shot to throw consistently, and without constant repetition it will hurt a bowler's average rather than help it. If you aspire to become a 180-average bowler, the straight ball is your best bet. To average better than 200, though, you just about have to throw the hook, because otherwise you won't get the strikes.

The drawings below show the starting finger and thumb positions on the three basic shots: the straight ball, shallow hook and large hook. Imagine the silhouette of the ball as a face of a clock in the release area.

The typical ball actions that will correspond to correctly thrown shots using those grips will look like this:

Straight Ball

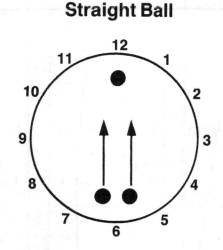

Shallow Hook   Large Hook

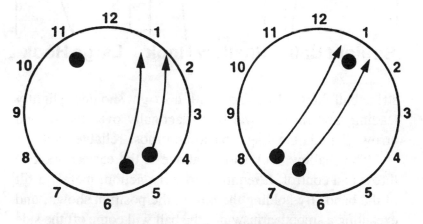

The straight ball should be held with the forearm facing up and the fingers facing six o'clock and the thumb facing twelve o'clock. The right-handed bowler should line up his

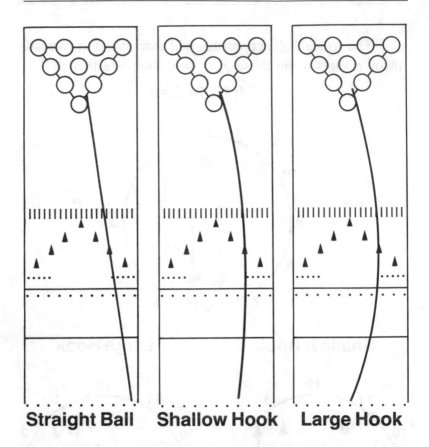

Straight Ball   Shallow Hook   Large Hook

strike ball facing the pocket with his right shoulder slightly leading, and throw towards it diagonally over the second arrow. This is bowling's basic and most reliable shot.

The shallow hook shown above is the easiest hook to throw and control. It requires no wrist action, merely a tilt of the hand. By holding the ball in the position shown, and executing a smooth armswing, the ball will come off the side of your hand at release, and hook between three and four inches before it reaches the pocket. You can throw it over the second arrow, just as you would a straight ball, but your body should be farther left on the approach, with your right shoulder facing the target, which will put your shoulder slightly back for right-handers. This is an excellent "starter" hook.

In the last figure shown above, we are talking about a serious hook, covering anywhere from six to eight inches on the lane. The ball is held with the wrist turned out. In the release, the finger action will start at seven o'clock and end at one o'clock. It is delivered just right of the center of the lane with strong finger rotation that will send it toward the channel before it curves back into the pocket. This shot requires a ball drilled with a semi-fingertip or fingertip grip and very strong wrist and fingers. It's the pros' shot, and mastering it—and keeping it mastered—is a full-time job.

There are many variations on the two hooks discussed above—too many to cover in a non-technical book like this. Experimentation will reveal them to you. People who have spent a lifetime in bowling, as I have, typically have thrown many kinds of shots over the years. I began, as a kid, as a straight-ball bowler using a conventionally drilled ball. From there I moved, on my own, to a shallow hook, and later, while still a teen, to a fingertip ball and a more-exaggerated hook. That was my basic shot until age and changing lane conditions forced me to simplify my stroke to throw a shot similar to the shallow hook illustrated above. The power-versus-control issue is the same among the pros as it is among recreational bowlers, only at a higher level of efficiency. Never lose sight of the fact that you always must sacrifice some of one to get more of the other.

Power and Speed

No book on bowling should fail to clear up a basic misconception many bowlers have about power and ball speed. They are not, repeat, not, synonymous. The harder a ball is thrown, the more it *slides*. Taken to an extreme, this can produce a shot that will not grip the lane sufficiently and will give you a lot of deflection in the pocket, reducing your pin count.

Some bowlers, of course, need more speed rather than less, because if you throw too slow the rotation on the ball will be eaten up by friction of the lane and the rotational energy will be lost. I'm talking mainly about youngsters and small women here. There are three main ways to increase ball speed: increase the height at which you hold the ball, which will give you a higher backswing and longer throwing arc; speed up your ·approach; or use a lighter ball. I recommend a longer armswing or lighter ball, because speeding up your approach tends to upset other parts of your delivery.

If you have the opposite problem—too much speed—hold the ball lower. That will lower your backswing and slow your delivery. I am talking mostly to large men here, who probably do and should use the maximum-weighted, 16-pound ball. It's most helpful, I think, to understand that bowling is a game of timing and rhythm, not sheer strength, and that practicing a *rhythmic* stroke will fight the tendency to overthrow. If you guys want to impress your buddies or girlfriends with your muscles, take them to a gym instead of a bowling center.

How to Practice at the Bowling Center

No improvement is possible without practice; I can't put it any simpler than that. By practice I mean bowling away from your usual competitive setting, be it league or tournament play. Only when you are freed from the necessity of rolling your best game for score can you experiment with the things that will improve your score in the long run.

It's not only necessary that you practice, but also that you do it correctly. Practice should be more than an occasional, idle game or two in which you try a little of this or a little of that. Here are some suggestions for making the most of your practice time.

At the bowling center, it's best to **practice with a friend** who knows bowling and also wants to improve his or her game. Your friend can act as your spotter, watching things you can't watch, such as the height of your backswing or the position of your body at various stages of your delivery. My wife, Ginny, does this for me very well. If you have no friend who's that perceptive, or only know people who want to fool around on the lanes, it's best that you avoid distractions by practicing alone.

Don't keep score. Scoring emphasizes rewards and penalties, and it has no place in a session devoted to doing the difficult things that may only pay off in the long run. Watch what you are doing and how your ball behaves when you try your adjustments, but forget about the numbers. Mark each frame you bowl with a check so you will know how much to pay when you're done.

Have a plan. Decide what part of your game needs work the most, and concentrate on it. If you are an occasional bowler, your spare-shooting probably should take top priority. Most people don't realize that the difference between going from a 170 to a 190 average is making two more spares a game. That usually can be done without making any basic changes in the way a person bowls. To go from the 190-

average level to the elite 210 class, a bowler must increase his strike average to more than six from four a game, and that often requires changing from a straight ball to a hook, or from a shallow hook to a large one. And that, in turn, requires more practice time than a non-professional may be willing or able to put in.

More bowling centers are facilitating spare practice by installing a computer-run device that will set any pattern of pins on the command of a ball-rack console. If your local center doesn't have one of these, you will have to practice picking off spares with the full rack of pins standing. That's not necessarily a handicap, though. If you can pick off just the seven or ten pin from the full rack, you surely can do it when they are alone. The same goes for most spare combinations.

The advanced bowler is best advised to practice grooving his strike ball, and learning to adapt his game to the different lane conditions he'll encounter when he travels. You may, for instance, normally roll your ball over the second arrow on the lanes in the bowling center you frequent, but you may go to a place where conditions won't permit you to do that successfully. Thus, you should devote some practice time to bowling over the first, third or fourth arrows. Learning which alternate routes you can handle—and which you can't—is valuable information to have when you encounter unforeseen circumstances.

Similarly, the advanced bowler should experiment with delivery tempos that differ from his normal one. Oily lanes sometimes require that you slow down your approach, not just for one or two shots, but for a whole evening. Conversely, a slow-tempo bowler may find that he must increase his approach speed to cope with dry lanes. If a bowler finds that he *can't* vary his tempo and still be effective, he is better off adding to his arsenal of high- or low-friction bowling balls that can aid him under "unfriendly" conditions. That's something else one should learn through practice.

Practicing at Home

Your practice needn't cease on weeks when you can't get to a bowling center except to bowl competitively. Here are some things you can do at home:

Mark off your approach distance on a wood floor or a rug or carpet, and go through your motion. If you have a polished wood floor of the appropriate length (15 or 16 feet), wear your bowling shoes. If you must use a covered surface, wear socks but no shoes.

Even if you have a wood floor at your disposal, it's good to rehearse your approach on a rug or carpet from time to time, as I do, wearing just socks on your feet. You'll have to tread lighter than you would wearing bowling shoes on wood, and if your feet dig in too deep on the rug, the way a lot of people's do on real lanes, you just might stick and fall. It's the opposite of the exercise baseball players get by swinging a heavy bat or iron bar in the on-deck circle before batting, but it can have the same, positive, effect.

It's my observation that many bowlers begin their approaches stiff-legged, with their trunks bent forward. You can practice counteracting this at home by taking a chair, putting the backs of your calves against the front of the chair, and lowering yourself into a sitting position. Sitting and rising a few times without using your hands will let you rehearse the bent-knee posture that's essential to a proper stance.

Another thing you can do at home is **practice your delivery in front of a mirror.** It may open your eyes to some differences between what you think you are doing on the lanes, and what you're actually doing.

When you watch yourself in the mirror, or in a back-lighted living room bay window that can serve the same purpose, check the various parts of your body for correct carriage. Is your head still and erect, as it should be, or is it cocked or bent down or forward? Is your trunk leaning slightly forward? Are your knees bent a bit? How high is your backswing? Is it above your shoulder only because your trunk and head are too far forward? And what about your hips: Are they parallel to the floor the way they should be? The mirror knows, and shows.

Do some eye exercises. Start a weight swinging from side to side at the end of a string, and practice following it with your eyes instead of by moving your head. Also practice up-and-down eye movements. Some bowlers dip their heads as they approach their targets, throwing off their deliveries. Practicing moving the eyes, not the head, will help correct this.

Practice your armswing. I wouldn't recommend you doing this with a bowling ball, because it can cause a lot of damage if you let it go. But common household items with handles, like a steam iron or a briefcase with some books in it, will do as well. Keep your grip firm but your arm muscles loose, and swing the object freely, back and forth. Using an object that's lighter than a bowling ball for this purpose will allow you to concentrate on fully extending your arm during the swing.

You probably can't actually bowl at home, but you can practice your ball release **on your bed.** That's right, your bed. Stand with your legs straight and your knees against the foot of the bed, and release your ball onto the mattress.

You'll be able to see if your ball is leaving your hand smoothly, without thumb drag. The exercise also should help cure you of lofting the ball, because if you loft it onto your bed often enough, you'll break the springs, and maybe some other things. I always do this drill a few times before leaving to bowl a tournament.

Some words of caution are in order here. Put heavy pillows or bolsters in front of your bed's headboard, so your ball won't wreck it. If you're in a hotel, or live in an apartment, it's probably also a good idea to put something along the sides of your bed to keep the ball from bouncing on the floor and disturbing the people downstairs. I'm sure that people in some of the hotels I've stayed in on the tour have wondered what the heck that crazy guy upstairs was up to.

10

Better Bowling:
Tactics

Knowing how to deliver a bowling ball properly is only part of the process of improving your game; you also must know how to adapt your stroke to the various lane conditions and pin "leaves" you will encounter. Indeed, the better you are, the more important the tactical side of the sport becomes. I think I can say without fear of contradiction that about 80 percent of the differences among bowlers on the pro tour are tactical rather than mechanical. Achieving a firm grasp of bowling tactics should add an immediate 10 pins to the novice's average, and it's a necessity for anyone aspiring to the elite levels of the sport.

Before getting specific, I think a few words about the difference between strategy and tactics are in order. The dictionary defines strategy in terms of large-scale operations (usually military, to be sure) with long-range objectives, while tactics are the immediate means to those ends. Your bowling strategy should always be *to knock down as many pins as you can in any situation.* The tactics you employ will dictate *how best the scoring will be done.*

The tournament that best exemplified this difference for me was the 1979 Miller High Life Classic that I won in Anaheim, California. As I noted in chapter 6, the lanes came up so slick for the Saturday TV final of that tourney that I had to bowl defensively. That meant that instead of putting full speed and spin on my first shots in search of strikes, which I almost always do, I took off something in the name of control and concentrated on staying around the headpin, so I could avoid the splits and railroads that lead to open frames. Maximizing my pin count remained my *strategy;* sacrificing my best strike ball was my *tactic.* The wisdom of that approach was seen in the fact that my first-game score of 204 was the only one that topped 200 for the afternoon, a rarity when five top-flight players turn in eight scores. I won because the other four guys in that final didn't adapt their games to the lane conditions. Their normal power shots skidded and slid into scores in the 170s and, even, 160s. They might have been as good mechanically as I was that day, but tactically I had 'em beat a mile.

Reading the Lanes

The first thing any bowler must do before he sets ball to lane is figure out what he's up against. As I've said before, the necessity to do this varies. Once-a-week league bowlers who always bowl on the same lanes can pretty much expect the same conditions week in and week out. Straight-ball bowlers can be less sensitive to lane-condition variations than hook-ball bowlers because their shots are less affected by such vicissitudes. (That's a strong reason occasional bowlers should stick with a straight ball rather than experimenting with hooks.) Lefties can pay less heed to lane-wear patterns than righties because only about 10 percent of all bowlers are southpaws, so their side is subject to a lot less wear and tear.

Some generalizations can be made about lane conditions, and they come under the heading of **sizing-up a bowling center.** Like most generalizations, they don't apply in all situations, but knowing them will at least give you a leg up. The more you bowl, and the more you travel, the more valuable they can be to you.

If you bowl much during non-league hours when many centers aren't full, you've probably noticed that the employees like to keep the lanes in front of their counters busiest. That way they can watch the action and handle problems with a minimum of effort. Usually, the counter is in the middle of the establishment, between lanes 18 and 22 in a 40-lane center, so you can assume that those lanes will get the most play and, naturally, suffer the most wear. Increased wear causes a lane's oil dressing to dissipate, or break down, more quickly. That, in turn, means that balls usually will hook more, and bowlers must adjust their shots accordingly to maintain their averages.

You also must beware of lanes near a center's doors, usually at the ends of the building. If it's cold out, the air coming in through the door will drop the temperature immediately inside and make the end lanes slicker. If it's hot, the warm air coming in will dry the oil on the nearest lanes and, generally, cause them to hook more.

Note, too, the position of the ball-return racks in relation to the lanes. Bowlers tend to shy away from the racks, so you can expect wear patterns on lanes that are to the *left* of the racks to be *closer to the center* than on lanes that are to the right of the racks, most people being right-handed. If you can overcome the fear of getting cozy with a ball rack, you'll often be able to find a smooth surface for your ball.

Your examination of the lanes should begin in earnest as soon as you arrive at your bowling center. Get there a bit early so you can watch other people bowl and see how their shots are reacting on the lanes to which you have been assigned. This works especially well if you can focus on an individual who displays above-average shot consistency, and whose game you know. Watch to see how much his shots are hooking, and compare it with what you've observed before. That ought to give you at least an idea of what's going on, especially if he's using his usual ball.

Next, of course, you'll want to closely examine the lanes themselves. The main things to look for are the shininess of the finish and the location and degree of wear in the ball track. Wear shows itself in a darkness of the boards on a lane, or through visible splintering or roughness caused by the action of ball against wood.

Generally speaking, a shiny lane is an oily one that will hook less than one with a drier, duller finish, but things can be more complicated than that. It's not my intention to go into great detail on all or even most of the different lane conditions you may encounter. That's more than the average, or, even, better-than-average bowler needs to know. You should be aware, though, that there are times shots can hook *sharper* on a shiny lane than on a dull one. That's because a shiny surface usually indicates a low-porosity base coat, and if there is heavy oil on top of that, the lane can be very slick. On the other hand, if the oil is scanty or there is no oil at all it also can accentuate hooking action.

Whatever the specifics, and you often must bowl a few frames on a lane to discover its true characteristics, you can look for strong ball reactions of all kinds on shiny lanes, and more variations as the oil from the front is carried to the rear during play. A duller-appearing surface usually means that oil will hold better than on shiny-coated lanes.

With rare exceptions, the ball track or wear on a lane will be between the second and third arrows from the right side, where most people bowl. It takes about two years of use to create a substantial track, and most lanes are resurfaced every three or four years, so a good portion of the nation's lanes have 'em. A smooth surface usually is easier to bowl on than a worn one, so I recommend that when lane wear is obvious and extreme, you position yourself a bit to the right of where you normally do (for right-handers, of course), and bowl from there.

One lane-wear situation deserves special note. In order to combat low scores (and disgruntled patrons) because of lanes that are excessively worn, some proprietors apply extra oil just to the left of the ball track so that it helps guide balls toward the pocket. This is known as a block. The ABC strongly frowns on this condition, as well it should. However, if it exists where you bowl, you have no alternative but to take advantage of it.

In most cases, your analysis of the conditions of the lanes you'll bowl on will come down to rolling a few balls yourself and seeing how they behave. It's unfortunate, but true, that most centers don't allow league bowlers an adequate warmup, if they allow any at all. Thus, your first few frames of play-for-score will have to double as your lab to diagnose lane conditions. Roll your normal shots and watch how they react, and make the necessary adjustments.

If a lane comes up slicker than usual, the most effective response is to move slightly to the right of where you normally bowl (for right-handers) and turn your body towards your target accordingly. This will involve leading more with your right shoulder than you usually do. Slow your approach a bit, giving your ball a better chance to "grab" the lane and hook.

On a drier-than-normal lane, you hook-ball bowlers should move toward the center of the lane and turn so that your left shoulder leads your body in the approach. Speed up your approach a bit to increase your ball speed, otherwise your shot will hook too soon and either miss the pocket on the high, or left, side, or lose its striking power.

An alternative is to change to a higher- or lower-friction bowling ball as conditions warrant. This approach sounds easy, but, in fact, coping with unusual lanes often requires *both* a change of ball and release. And because lane conditions can change while you are bowling, the ability to vary your delivery through practice is a necessary part of getting your scoring average into the expert class.

Pin Targeting

The next point about bowling tactics that should be understood is the correct spot on the pin, or pins, for which to aim; in other words, you must know the location of your *true* target. This might be old stuff for expert readers, but the fact that the true center of a pin on almost all shots isn't the center of the pin *as you face it from the foul line,* hasn't been fully realized by many novice or occasional bowlers.

The example that most easily illustrates the point is the proper target for the first ball: the 1-3 pocket from which most strikes come. Some people might think it useful to visualize rolling the ball exactly in the center of where those two pins stand, but I don't. What you'll see there is mostly air. I find it better to target my strike ball on the "true center" of the headpin.

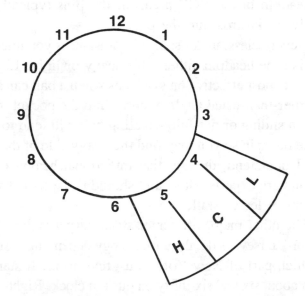

I find it useful to think of the round bottom of the head pin—and others as well—as clock-faces, and identify target areas as one might tell time. The center of the pin as you face the foul line is at six o'clock, but that shouldn't be your strike target when you bowl. The pin's real center, marked with "C" in the drawing above, is between four and five o'clock for right handers, or seven and eight o'clock for lefties. That's the spot that will produce the best pin action— and the most strikes—about 90 percent of the time. Hit it squarely and you'll rarely go wrong.

The other two areas marked on the drawing occupy the five to five-thirty and three-thirty to four o'clock spaces. They are marked "H" for the "high" or "heavy" side, and "L" for the "light" side. It is possible to get strikes after hitting the headpin in those places, but it's tougher because in most cases pins must rebound off the lane's sideboards before striking and toppling other pins, whereas when a ball hits the headpin in the "C" area, all the pins typically crash cleanly backwards into the pit.

Nevertheless, under some circumstances you might want to strike the headpin either a bit heavy or light. Light-side shots are most effective on dry lanes when a ball can achieve a sharper-than-usual angle of entry into the pocket. On oily lanes, a sliding or not-fully-rotating ball will tend to deflect off the headpin so you may find the heavy side of the pocket best. Understand, though, that intentional heavy- or light-side hits are experts' shots and shouldn't be trifled with by bowlers of lesser skill.

The other major off-center strike target is the "Brooklyn" or "Jersey" side, the terminology depending, I suppose, on which part of New York you grew up in. It stands between about six and six-thirty on our pin clock. Right-handers that strike the headpin on the "Brooklyn" side rarely get strikes because the right-to-left rotation of their ball is working away from the central pin mass rather than into it, as in the true-center hit, and the five and five-nine-pin "leaves" are typical. Straight-ball bowlers have better luck with Brooklyn-side strikes; I'd put their success rate at, maybe, 20 or 25 percent. Still, it's not a shot you can depend on, and not worth developing.

The same principle of true-center pin targeting that works on your strike ball also should apply to your spare shots.

The drawing below illustrates a right-hander's proper targets and angles of approach on three key, single-pin spares. It's especially important to understand proper targeting when going after the seven and ten pins. Trying to hit them in the center of the pin parallel to the lane is a good way to produce a channel ball.

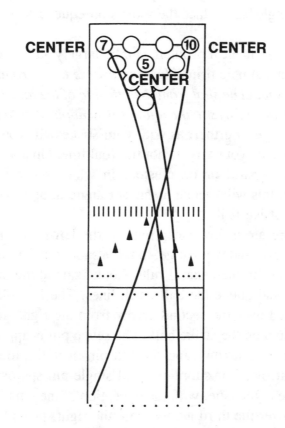

Spare Shooting

The single factor that keeps most ordinary bowlers ordinary is their failure to consistently convert makeable spares. Three things contribute most to this problem; one mechanical, one tactical, and one psychological. The mechanical one is the failure to line up properly in relation to the pins that are standing. The tactical one is the failure to identify the *real* target in spare clusters. The psychological one is that, on multiple-pin spare attempts, the mind sometimes boggles at the thought of having to knock down all of a group of pins with a single ball or face the score consequences of an open frame.

The mechanical problem can be largely addressed with a short and simple principle: *Any spares to the right of the headpin should be shot from the left side of the lane by right handers, and spares to the left of the headpin should be shot from the right.* Further, as with your strike ball, you should line up facing your target, not the foul line. On a seven-pin or ten-pin spare, or on clusters in which those pins are standing, this will dictate a sharper angle of approach than on your strike ball.

There are a few exceptions to the left-right principle stated above, and we will get to them soon, but for now let's concentrate on the general rule. Look again at the previous drawing and notice the ball-track lines. The five-pin spare is attacked over the second arrow from the right, just like the headpin on the strike ball. The seven pin is approached over the third arrow, and the ten pin over the fourth (or center) arrow. For simplicity, all single-pin spares on the right side of the lane, with the exception of the ten pin, may be shot over the third arrow from the right, providing you approach them from the left side of the lane and face your target. All single-pin spares on the left can be shot over the same arrow, with the approach starting from the right side of the lane and, again, angled toward the pin.

The exceptions to the left-right rule are illustrated below.

In these three, two-pin spare groups, the danger is in "chopping" one pin and leaving the other standing. The drawings show the proper ball lines for these spares. Note, for example, that the five-nine spare, the one that's frequently left when a first ball hits the headpin on the "Brooklyn" side, is approached over the *third* arrow from the right. Shooting this spare from the right as the majority of novices do, would result in picking off, or chopping, the five pin and leaving the nine. The other drawings illustrate the same principle. On all three, straight-ball bowlers should take slightly *shallower* angles than hook-ball bowlers.

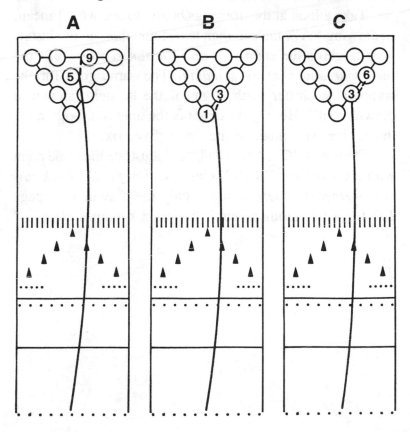

Spare clusters are easier to make if you adopt the tactical principle of selecting a *key pin* in every group. This makes the spare easier to *see,* and, psychologically, easier to convert, because your main concern is with knocking down just one pin, not several.

Nine out of ten times, the key pin in a cluster will be a pin in the back row, usually the eight or nine pin. Almost any cluster to the right of the headpin can be made by drawing an imaginary line to the nine-pin *whether it is standing or not.* The same holds for the eight-pin for clusters to the left of the headpin.

Take a look at the drawings below to see what I mean. In drawing "A", the common two, four, five, eight cluster, your target is the eight. *It's also the target when only the two, four and five are standing.* The same goes for the comparable cluster to the right of the headpin, shown in drawing "B". Here, your target is the nine-pin, both in the three, five, six, nine, or the three, five, six.

Drawings "C", "D", and "E" illustrate the same point with the so-called "fence" clusters. *Aim for the back-row pin whether it's there or not.* Study the drawings on page 207 for a few moments until the point becomes clear.

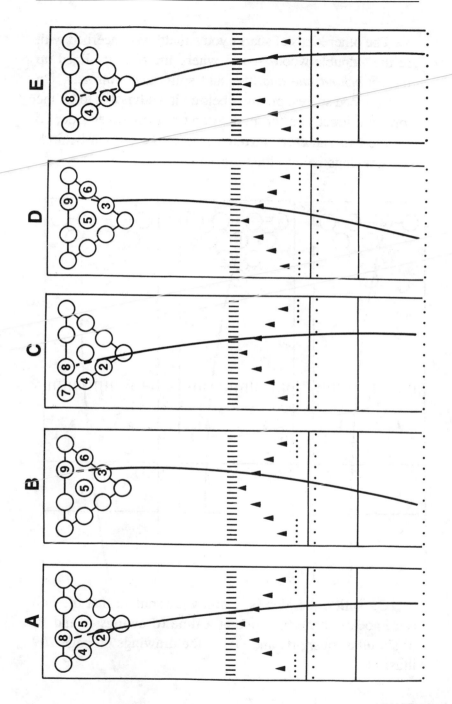

The other kinds of spares you should be concerned with are the "double wood" ones, where the pins are lined up *directly behind one another,* and splits and railroads. On double-wood spares, pictured below, it's advisable to hit the front pin directly in the middle and not on either side, so that the ball can carry through it to strike the pin behind. The drawings below illustrate.

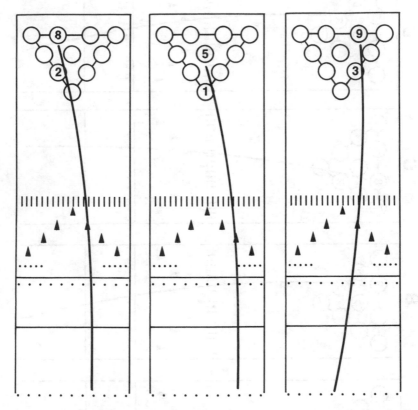

On **splits,** the idea is to aim your shot so that the ball can knock out the pins one at a time (drawings A and B) or simultaneously (C and D), as the drawings on page 209 illustrate.

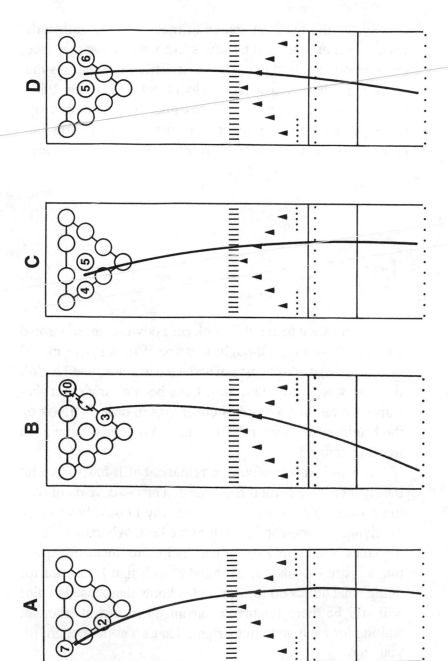

By far the toughest spares to make are the **railroads** where a pin or pins must be struck in a way so that *they* take out a second or third pin. The most difficult of these is the seven-ten. I left out a suggested ball track in diagram "D" because, really, it's next to impossible. So just throw, try to nudge one pin in the direction of the other, and pray the lights go out before your ball reaches the end of the lane.

* * * * *

I don't want to end this book on a down-note, so instead I'll leave you with a thought that Joe Wilman gave me 30 or so years ago. We'd just bowled a tournament, and I hadn't done very well. My chin must have been on my chest, because Joe felt that a word of cheer was in order. "Look on the bright side, Carmen," he said. "You could have been *working* today."

It wasn't that profound a remark, but it must have hit me right because I still remember it. Thirty-six years of rolling bowling balls wasn't the worst way I could have made my living. In fact, I still rank it as the best. Whenever I leave the lanes wishing my strike ball had more juice, or regretting a spare I'd missed, I remind myself that I get paid for doing what others do for fun. I also know that those ten pins will still be there tomorrow, arranged in a neat triangle, waiting for me to get things right. That's a good thought for you, too.

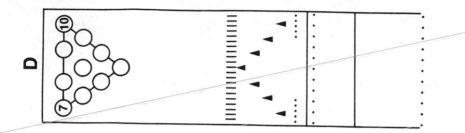

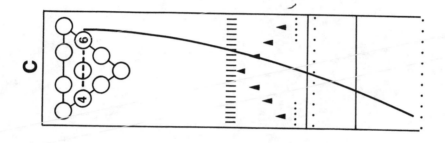

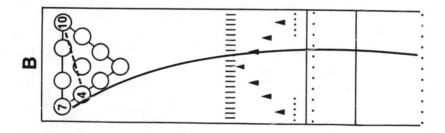

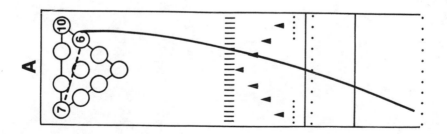

Carmen Salvino
Titles and Awards

Professional Bowlers Association Titles

1984—National Seniors Championship, Canton, Ohio
1979—Miller High Life Classic, Anaheim, California
1977—Houston Open, Houston, Texas
1976—Quad Cities Open, Davenport, Iowa
1975—Pittsburgh Open, No. Versailles, Pennsylvania
1975—Showboat Invitational, Las Vegas, Nevada
1974—New Jersey Open, Edison, New Jersey
1973—Lincoln-Mercury Open, New Orleans, Louisiana
1968—Caracas Invitational, Caracas, Venezuela
1967—Mobile Open, Mobile, Alabama
1967—St. Paul Open, St. Paul, Minnesota
1965—Birmingham Open, Birmingham, Alabama
1965—Paramus Open, Paramus, New Jersey
1964—Rockford Open, Rockford, Illinois
1963—Jacksonville Open, Jacksonville, Florida
1962—U.S. Nationals, Philadelphia, Pennsylvania
1962—Pontiac Open, Pontiac, Michigan
1961—Empire State Open, Albany, New York

Other Major Titles

1972—American Bowling Congress National Doubles
     (with Barry Asher)
1960 and 1954—Member, Championship Teams, Chi-
     cago Classic League
1957 and 1954—Chicago Individual Match Game
     Champion
1956—Illinois State All-Events Champion
1955—Petersen Masters Round Robin Champion

1954—Member, Tri-Par Radio, ABC National Team
    Champions
1952—Bowling Proprietors Association of America Na-
    tional Doubles (with Joe Wilman)
1952—Dom DeVito Classic Singles Champion

Honors

1985—Elected, Italian-American Sports Hall of Fame
1980—Elected, Chicago Sports Hall of Fame
1979—Elected, ABC Hall of Fame
1975—Elected, PBA Hall of Fame
1974—Elected, Illinois Bowling Association Hall of
    Fame
1985-86—Elected, President of the PBA
1985-86—Elected, Vice President, ABC Hall of Fame
    Board
1987-88—Elected, President, ABC Hall of Fame Board

Bowling Magazine All-American Team

First Team—1976
Second Team—1963, 1967, 1973, 1974

Bowlers Journal All-American Team

First Team—1975

PBA Records (as of January 1, 1987)

Most Career Tournaments—680
Most Top–24 Finishes—287
Most Career Cashes—459

Index

Swayda, Dennis, 105

T

Tactics, 195
  versus strategy, 195-96
Team bowling, 26, 31-33, 121-22
Toscanini, Arturo, 180
Tountas, Pete, 122
Tournaments
  See Dom DeVito Classic;
  Firestone Tournament of
  Champions; Miller High Life
  Classics; etc.

V

Varipapa, Andy, 19, 98-99
Venezuela
  See Salvino, Carmen, in
  Venezuela
Venezuela, Invitational (1968),
  89-90

W

Wagner, Chuck, 42, 70-71
Weber, Dick, 30, 77, 79, 82, 85,
  89-90, 111, 114, 129-30, 133,
  134-35, 167
Weber, Dick "Rich," Jr., 129
Weber, Johnny, 129
Weber, Pete, 129-30, 134
Welu, Billy, 77, 89, 93-94
Williams, Walter Ray, Jr., 115,
  130-31, 134
Wilman Joe, xiv, 26, 36, 39-41,
  42, 43, 71, 127, 134
Wilson, "Whispering Joe," 73
Wise, Bernie, 128-29
Woodman, Leon, 66

Y

Young, George, 40